THE
QUESTION OF
LAY ANALYSIS

By SIGMUND FREUD

THE STANDARD EDITION
OF THE COMPLETE PSYCHOLOGICAL WORKS OF
SIGMUND FREUD
24 VOLUMES

Sigmund Freud

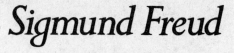

THE QUESTION OF
LAY ANALYSIS

Conversations with an Impartial Person

TRANSLATED AND EDITED BY
James Strachey

WITH A BIOGRAPHICAL
INTRODUCTION BY
Peter Gay

W·W· NORTON & COMPANY
New York · London

W. W. Norton & Company, Inc. is also the publisher of The Standard
Edition of the Complete Psychological Works of Sigmund Freud.

W. W. Norton & Company, Inc.
500 Fifth Avenue, New York, N.Y. 10110
www.wwnorton.com

W. W. Norton & Company Ltd.
Castle House, 75/76 Wells Street, London W1T 3QT

PRINTED IN THE UNITED STATES OF AMERICA

4 5 6 7 8 9 0

Contents

SIGMUND FREUD: A BRIEF LIFE

by Peter Gay

It was Freud's fate, as he observed not without pride, to "agitate the sleep of mankind." Half a century after his death, it seems clear that he succeeded far better than he expected, though in ways he would not have appreciated. It is commonplace but true that we all speak Freud now, correctly or not. We casually refer to oedipal conflicts and sibling rivalry, narcissism and Freudian slips. But before we can speak that way with authority, we must read his writings attentively. They repay reading, with dividends.

Sigmund Freud was born on May 6, 1856, in the small Moravian town of Freiberg.[1] His father, Jacob Freud, was an impecunious merchant; his mother, Amalia, was handsome, self-assertive, and young—twenty years her husband's junior and his third wife. Jacob Freud had two sons from his first marriage who were about Amalia Freud's age and lived nearby. One of these half brothers had a son, John, who, though Sigmund Freud's nephew, was older than his uncle.

---

[1]His given names were Sigismund Schlomo, but he never used his middle name and, after experimenting with the shorter form for some time, definitively adopted the first name Sigmund—on occasion relapsing into the original formulation—in the early 1870s, when he was a medical student at the University of Vienna. Freiberg, now in Czechoslovakia, bears the Czech name "Pribor."

Freud's family constellation, then, was intricate enough to puzzle the clever and inquisitive youngster. Inquisitiveness, the natural endowment of children, was particularly marked in him. Life would provide ample opportunity to satisfy it.

In 1860, when Freud was almost four, he moved with his family to Vienna, then a magnet for many immigrants. This was the opening phase of the Hapsburg Empire's liberal era. Jews, only recently freed from onerous taxes and humiliating restrictions on their property rights, professional choices, and religious practices, could realistically harbor hopes for economic advancement, political participation, and a measure of social acceptance. This was the time, Freud recalled, when "every industrious Jewish school boy carried a Cabinet Minister's portfolio in his satchel."[2] The young Freud was encouraged to cultivate high ambitions. As his mother's first-born and a family favorite, he secured, once his family could afford it, a room of his own. He showed marked gifts from his first school days, and in his secondary school, or Gymnasium, he was first in his class year after year.

In 1873, at seventeen, Freud entered the University of Vienna. He had planned to study law, but, driven on by what he called his "greed for knowledge," instead matriculated in the faculty of medicine, intending to embark, not on a conventional career as a physician, but on philosophical-scientific investigations that might solve some of the great riddles that fascinated him. He found his work in physiology and neurology so absorbing that he did not take his degree until 1881.

A brilliant researcher, he cultivated the habit of close observation and the congenial stance of scientific skepticism. He was privileged to work under professors with international reputations, almost all German imports and tough-

---

[2] *The Interpretation of Dreams* (1900), *SE* IV, 193.

minded positivists who disdained metaphysical speculations about, let alone pious explanations of, natural phenomena. Even after Freud modified their theories of the mind—in essence barely disguised physiological theories—he recalled his teachers with unfeigned gratitude. The most memorable of them, Ernst Brücke, an illustrious physiologist and a civilized but exacting taskmaster, confirmed Freud's bent as an unbeliever. Freud had grown up with no religious instruction at home, came to Vienna University as an atheist, and left it as an atheist—with persuasive scientific arguments.

In 1882, on Brücke's advice, Freud reluctantly left the laboratory to take a lowly post at the Vienna General Hospital. The reason was romantic: in April, he had met Martha Bernays, a slender, attractive young woman from northern Germany visiting one of his sisters, and fallen passionately in love. He was soon secretly engaged to her, but too poor to establish the respectable bourgeois household that he and his fiancée thought essential. It was not until September 1886, some five months after opening his practice in Vienna, with the aid of wedding gifts and loans from affluent friends, that the couple could marry. Within nine years, they had six children, the last of whom, Anna, grew up to be her father's confidante, secretary, nurse, disciple, and representative, and an eminent psychoanalyst in her own right.

Before his marriage, from October 1885 to February 1886, Freud worked in Paris with the celebrated French neurologist Jean-Martin Charcot, who impressed Freud with his bold advocacy of hypnosis as an instrument for healing medical disorders, and no less bold championship of the thesis (then quite unfashionable) that hysteria is an ailment to which men are susceptible no less than women. Charcot, an unrivaled observer, stimulated Freud's growing interest in the theoretical and therapeutic aspects of mental healing. Nervous ailments became Freud's specialty, and in the 1890s, as he told a friend, psychology became his tyrant. During these years he founded the psychoanalytic theory of mind.

He had intriguing if somewhat peculiar help. In 1887, he had met a nose-and-throat specialist from Berlin, Wilhelm Fliess, and rapidly established an intimate friendship with him. Fliess was the listener the lonely Freud craved: an intellectual gambler shocked at no idea, a propagator of provocative (at times fruitful) theories, an enthusiast who fed Freud ideas on which he could build. For over a decade, Fliess and Freud exchanged confidential letters and technical memoranda, meeting occasionally to explore their subversive notions. And Freud was propelled toward the discovery of psychoanalysis in his practice: his patients proved excellent teachers. He was increasingly specializing in women suffering from hysteria, and, observing their symptoms and listening to their complaints, he found that, though a good listener, he did not listen carefully enough. They had much to tell him.

In 1895, Freud and his fatherly friend Josef Breuer, a thriving, generous internist, published *Studies on Hysteria*, assigning Breuer's former patient "Anna O." pride of place. She had furnished fascinating material for intimate conversations between Breuer and Freud, and was to become, quite against her—and Breuer's—will, the founding patient of psychoanalysis. She demonstrated to Freud's satisfaction that hysteria originates in sexual malfunctioning and that symptoms can be talked away.

The year 1895 was decisive for Freud in other ways. In July, Freud managed to analyze a dream, his own, fully. He would employ this dream, known as "Irma's injection," as a model for psychoanalytic dream interpretation when he published it, some four years later, in his *Interpretation of*

Dreams. In the fall, he drafted, but neither completed nor published, what was later called the Project for a Scientific Psychology. It anticipated some of his fundamental theories yet serves as a reminder that Freud had been deeply enmeshed in the traditional physiological interpretation of mental events.

Increasingly Freud was offering psychological explanations for psychological phenomena. In the spring of 1896, he first used the fateful name, "psychoanalysis." Then in October his father died; "the most important event," he recalled a dozen years later, "the most poignant loss, of a man's life."[3] It supplied a powerful impetus toward psychoanalytic theorizing, stirring Freud to his unprecedented self-analysis, more systematic and thoroughgoing than the frankest autobiographer's self-probing. In the next three or four years, as he labored over his "Dream book," new discoveries crowded his days. But first he had to jettison the "seduction theory" he had championed for some time. It held that *every* neurosis results from premature sexual activity, mainly child molestation, in childhood.[4] Once freed from this far-reaching but improbable theory, Freud could appreciate the share of fantasies in mental life, and discover the Oedipus complex, that universal family triangle.

Freud's *Interpretation of Dreams* was published in November 1899.[5] It treated all dreams as wish fulfillments, detailed the mental stratagems that translate their causes into the strange drama the awakening dreamer remembers,

---

[3]Ibid., xxvi.

[4]Freud never claimed that sexual abuse does not exist. He had patients who he knew had not imagined the assaults they reported. All he abandoned when he abandoned the seduction theory was the sweeping claim that *only* the rape of a child, whether a boy or a girl, by a servant, an older sibling, or a classmate, could be the cause of a neurosis.

[5]The book bears the date of 1900 on the title page and this date is usually given as the date of publication.

and, in the difficult seventh chapter, outlined a comprehensive theory of mind. Its first reception was cool. During six years, only 351 copies were sold; a second edition did not appear until 1909. However, Freud's popularly written *Psychopathology of Everyday Life* of 1901 found a wider audience. Its collection of appealing slips of all sorts made Freud's fundamental point that the mind, however disheveled it might appear, is governed by firm rules. Thus—to give but one typical instance—the presiding officer of the Austrian parliament, facing a disagreeable season, opened it with the formal declaration that it was hereby closed. That "accident" had been prompted by his hidden repugnance for the sessions ahead.

Gradually, though still considered a radical, Freud acquired prestige and supporters. He had quarreled with Fliess in 1900, and, though their correspondence lingered on for some time, the two men never met again. Yet in 1902, after unconscionable delays, apparently generated by anti-Semitism combined with distrust of the maverick innovator, he was finally appointed an associate professor at the University of Vienna. Late that year, Freud and four other Viennese physicians began meeting every Wednesday night in his apartment at Berggasse 19 to discuss psychoanalytic questions; four years after, the group, grown to over a dozen regular participants, employed a paid secretary (Otto Rank) to take minutes and keep records. Finally, in 1908, it was transformed into the Vienna Psychoanalytic Society. At least some medical men (and a few women) were taking Freud's ideas seriously.

In 1905, Freud buttressed the structure of psychoanalytic thought with the second pillar of his theory: the *Three Essays on the Theory of Sexuality.* It outlined perversions and "normal" development from childhood to puberty with a lack of censoriousness and an openness hitherto virtually unknown in medical literature. Again in 1905, Freud brought out his book on jokes and the first of his famous case histories: "Fragment of an Analysis of a Case of Hysteria," nicknamed the "Dora case." He published it to illustrate the uses of dream interpretation in psychoanalysis, and expose his failure to recognize the power of transference in the analytic situation, but its lack of empathy with his embattled teen-age analysand has made it controversial.

In the following decade, Freud enriched the technique of psychoanalysis with three more sophisticated case histories—"Analysis of a Phobia in a Five-Year-Old Boy" ("Little Hans"), "Notes upon a Case of Obsessional Neurosis" ("Rat Man") in 1909, and "Psycho-Analytic Notes on an Autobiographical Account of a Case of Paranoia" ("Schreber Case") in 1911. Despite recent reanalyses, they remain lucid expository models across a wide spectrum of mental ailments. Then, from 1910 on, Freud published pioneering, exceedingly influential papers on technique, to establish psychoanalytic method on sound foundations. Nor did he neglect theory; witness such an important paper as "Formulations on the Two Principles of Mental Functioning" (1911), in which he differentiated between the "primary process," the primitive, unconscious element in the mind, and the "secondary process," largely conscious and controlled.

During these years, Freud also broke out of the circumscribed bounds of clinical and theoretical specialization by publishing papers on religion, literature, sexual mores, biography, sculpture, prehistory, and much else. "Obsessive Actions and Religious Practices" (1907), "Creative Writers and Daydreaming" (1908), " 'Civilized' Sexual Morality and Modern Nervous Illness" (1908), and his widely debated study of the origins of homosexuality, "Leonardo da Vinci and a Memory of His Childhood" (1910), are only samples of his range. Freud took all of culture as his prov-

ince. He was realizing the program he had outlined for
himself in his youth: to solve some of the great riddles of
human existence.

Yet Freud also found the decade from 1905 to 1914
agitating with the progress of, and disagreeable splits within,
a rapidly emerging international movement—*his* movement. Psychoanalytic politics took center stage. Two principal sources of hope for the future of Freud's ideas, and later
of envenomed contention, were the intelligent, Socialist
Viennese physician Alfred Adler (1870–1937), and the original, self-willed Swiss psychiatrist Carl G. Jung (1875–1961).
Adler had been among Freud's earliest adherents and remained for some years his most prominent Viennese advo-
cate. But as professional interest in psychoanalysis—not all
of it benevolent—grew apace, as Freud's upsetting ideas
were being explored at psychiatrists' congresses, Freud as-
pired to enlarge the reach of psychoanalysis beyond its place
of origin. Vienna, with its handful of followers, struck him
as provincial, unsuitable as headquarters.

The first breakthrough came in 1906, when Jung, then
principal psychiatrist at the renowned clinic Burghölzli in
Zurich, sent Freud an offprint. Freud responded promptly;
a cordial correspondence blossomed, and the friendship was
cemented by Jung's visit to Freud in early 1907. Freud was
only fifty, vigorous and productive, but he had long brooded
on himself as aging and decrepit. He was seeking a successor
who would carry the psychoanalytic dispensation to later
generations and into a world larger than the Viennese, Jewish ambiance to which psychoanalysis was then confined.
Jung, a formidable presence and energetic debater, was an
inspired discovery: he was not old, he was not Viennese, he
was not Jewish. Jung was prominent in the first international
congress of psychoanalysts at Salzburg in the spring of 1908,
and was appointed, the following year, editor of a newly

founded *Yearbook.* Freud, delighted with Jung, anointed
him his son, his crown prince—accolades that Jung welcomed, indeed encouraged. Hence, when the International
Psychoanalytic Association was founded in March 1910, in
Nürnberg, Jung was Freud's logical, inevitable, choice for
president. Freud's Viennese adherents saw their city dis-
placed by Zurich as the center of psychoanalysis, and did not
like it. A compromise was hammered out, and for some time
peace reigned in the Vienna Psychoanalytic Society. But
Adler was developing distinctive psychological ideas, which
featured aggressiveness over sexuality, and "organ inferior-
ity" as a dominant cause of neuroses. A split became inevitable, and, in the summer of 1911, Adler and some of his
adherents resigned, leaving Freud and the Freudians in control of the Vienna society.

Freud was not without accolades. In September 1909, he
had received an honorary doctorate at Clark University in
Worcester, Massachusetts, as had Jung. But like Adler, Jung
increasingly diverged from Freud's ideas. He had never been
easy with the prominence Freud assigned to the sexual
drive—libido. By early 1912, these reservations took a personal turn. In response, Ernest Jones, Freud's principal English lieutenant, formed a defensive secret band of like-
minded analysts, the Committee. It consisted of himself,
Freud, Sandor Ferenczi (a brilliant adherent from Budapest), the witty Viennese lawyer Hanns Sachs, the astute
Berlin clinician and theorist Karl Abraham, and Freud's
amanuensis, the autodidact Otto Rank. It seemed needed:
by late 1912, the correspondence between Jung and Freud
had grown acrimonious and in January 1914, Freud ter-
minated his friendship with Jung. A split was only a matter
of time; in the spring of 1914, Jung resigned from his powerful positions in the psychoanalytic movement.

The strains of psychoanalytic politics did not keep Freud

from continuing his explorations of an impressive variety of topics. In 1913, he published an audacious, highly speculative venture into psychoanalytic prehistory, *Totem and Taboo,* which specified the moment that savages, in some dim, remote past, entered culture by murdering their father and acquiring guilt feelings. Then, in 1914, he published (anonymously) "The Moses of Michelangelo," uniting his admiration for Michelangelo's brooding sculpture with his powers of observation. In the same year, with an unsettling paper on narcissism, he subverted crucial aspects of psychoanalytic thought by throwing doubts upon his theory of drives—hitherto divided into erotic and egoistic.

But harrowing events on the world stage shouldered aside Freud's reassessment of psychoanalytic theory. On June 28, 1914, Austria's Archduke Francis Ferdinand and his consort were assassinated. Six weeks later, on August 4, Europe was at war. The first casualty for psychoanalysis was Freud's eventually best-known case history, "From the History of an Infantile Neurosis" ("Wolf Man"), written in the fall of 1914, but not published until 1918. Psychoanalytic activity almost ground to a halt. Many potential patients were at the front; most psychoanalysts were drafted into the medical corps; communications between "enemies" like Ernest Jones and Freud were severely truncated; psychoanalytic publications almost vanished; and congresses, the lifeblood of communication, were out of the question. For Freud, these were anxious times in other ways: all three of his sons were in the army, two of them almost daily in mortal danger.

Yet the war did not idle Freud's mind. Having too much time on his hands, he used it to good purpose. Work was a defense against brooding. Between March and July 1915, he wrote a dozen fundamental papers on metapsychology—on the unconscious, on repression, on melancholia; but he refused to gather them into the basic textbook he had planned. He published five of the papers between 1915 and 1917, and destroyed the rest. His enigmatic dissatisfaction with them hints at the discontent that had fueled his paper on narcissism.. His map of the mind was inadequate to the evidence he had accumulated in his clinical experience. But he still lacked a satisfactory alternative. That would have to wait until after the war.

Another wartime activity, though more successful, gave Freud only modest pleasure: beginning in 1915, he delivered lectures at the university, published as a single volume in 1917 as *Introductory Lectures on Psycho-Analysis*. With the cunning of the born popularizer, Freud opened with a series on ordinary experiences, slips of the tongue, "unmotivated" forgetting, then turned to dreams and concluded with the technical topic, neuroses. Frequently reprinted and widely translated, these *Introductory Lectures* finally secured Freud a wide audience.

The war dragged on. Originally, somewhat to his surprise, an Austrian patriot, Freud wearied of the endless slaughter. He grew appalled at the chauvinism of intellectuals, the callousness of commanders, the stupidity of politicians. He had not yet fully acknowledged the theoretical significance of aggression, even though psychoanalysts had regularly encountered aggressiveness among their patients. But the war, beastly as it was, confirmed the skeptical psychoanalytic appraisal of human nature.

Signs of revived activity came shortly before the end of hostilities. In September 1918, for the first time since 1913, psychoanalysts from Germany and Austria-Hungary met in Budapest. Two months later, the war was over. To the family's immense relief, all of Freud's sons survived it. But the time for worry was far from over. The defeated powers were faced with revolution, drastically transformed from empires into republics, and saddled with stringent, vindictive peace treaties stripping them of territory and resources. Vienna was hungry, cold, desperate; food and fuel shortages produced deadly ailments—tuberculosis and influenza. In this stressful situation, Freud, who wasted no tears on the departed Hapsburg Empire, proved an energetic, imaginative manager. The portrait of Martha Freud shielding Herr Professor from domestic realities needs revision. Freud dispatched precise requests abroad to relatives, friends, associates, specifying what nourishment and clothing his family needed most, and how to send packages safely. Then, in January 1920, postwar misery struck home with deadly force: Freud's beloved second daughter Sophie, married and living in Hamburg, mother of two children, died in the influenza epidemic.

It has been plausibly argued that her death suggested the pessimistic drive theory that Freud now developed. Actually, he had virtually completed *Beyond the Pleasure Principle* (1920), which first announced Freud's theory of the death drive, the year before. Once Freud had adopted this construct, in which the forces of life, Eros, dramatically confront the forces of death, Thanatos, he found himself unable to think any other way. In 1923, in his classic study *The Ego and the Id,* he completed his revisions. He now proposed a "structural theory" of the mind, which visualizes the mind as divided into three distinct yet interacting agencies: the id (the wholly unconscious domain of the mind, consisting of the drives and of material later repressed), the ego (which is partly conscious and contains the defense mechanisms and the capacities to calculate, reason, and plan), and the super-ego (also only partly conscious, which harbors the conscience and, beyond that, unconscious feelings of guilt). This new scheme did not lead Freud to abandon his classic characterization of mental activity—emphasizing the distance of thoughts from awareness—as either conscious, or preconscious, or wholly unconscious. But he now made the decisive point that many of the mental operations of the ego, and of the super-ego as well, are inaccessible to direct introspection.

Meanwhile, the psychoanalytic movement was flourishing. Freud was becoming a household word, though he detested the sensationalized attention the popular press gave him. Better: in 1920, at the first postwar congress at The Hague, former "enemies" met as friends. Freud was accompanied by his daughter Anna, whom he was then analyzing and who joined the Vienna Psychoanalytic Society in 1922. In that year, the analysts convened in Berlin. It was the last congress Freud ever attended. In April 1923, he was operated on for a growth in his palate. While for months his doctors and closest associates pretended that the growth was benign, by September the truth was out: he had cancer. Severe operations followed in the fall. From then on Freud, compelled to wear a prosthesis, was rarely free of discomfort or pain.

But he never stopped working. While he had trouble speaking, he continued to analyze patients, many of them American physicians who came to Vienna as his "pupils" and returned to analyze in New York or Chicago. He continued to revise his theories. From the mid-1920s on, he wrote controversial papers on female sexuality, and, in 1926, *Inhibitions, Symptoms, and Anxiety,* which reversed his earlier thinking on anxiety, now treating it as a danger signal. Moreover, he wrote essays that found a relatively wide public: *The Future of an Illusion,* a convinced atheist's dissection of religion, in 1927, and, in 1930, *Civilization and Its Discontents,* a disillusioned look at modern civilization on the verge of catastrophe.

In 1933, that catastrophe came. On January 30, Hitler was appointed chancellor in Germany, and from then on

Austrian Nazis, already active, increasingly intervened in politics. The old guard was disappearing: Karl Abraham had died prematurely in 1925; Sandor Ferenczi followed him in 1933. Freud's closest friends were gone. But Freud was unwilling to leave the Vienna he hated and loved: he was too old, he did not want to desert, and besides, the Nazis would never invade his country. On the morning of March 12, 1938, the Germans proved him wrong. As the Nazis marched in, a jubilant populace greeted them. Spontaneous anti-Semitic outrages surpassed anything Germans had witnessed after five years of Nazi rule. Late in March, Anna was summoned to Gestapo headquarters; while she was released unharmed, the trauma changed Freud's mind: he must emigrate. It took months to satisfy the Nazi government's extortions, but on June 4, Freud left for Paris, welcomed by his former analysand and loving disciple, Princess Marie Bonaparte. On June 6, Freud landed in London, preceded by most of his family, "to die in freedom."

Aged and ill, he kept on working. Freud's last completed book, *Moses and Monotheism,* irritated and dismayed his Jewish readers with its assertion that Moses had been an Egyptian: he ended life as he had lived it—a disturber of the peace. He died bravely on September 23, 1939, asking his physician for a lethal dose of morphine. Freud did not believe in personal immortality, but his work lives on.

About This Book

Even before the First World War, while he was in the early phase of organizing his supporters into a coherent psychoanalytic movement, Freud had insisted that a medical education was not necessarily useful to, and might even impede, the psychoanalyst. As a trained physician and medical researcher, Freud was in a secure position to argue that point forcefully. But he found strenuous resistance among even his most pliant followers on this issue, particularly in the United States. American psychoanalysts, beset by charlatans who could easily set up shop as mental healers, were persuaded that a doctor's shingle could serve as a guarantee of respectability and reliability. When, in 1926, the authorities in Vienna proceeded against Theodor Reik, one of Freud's younger adherents whom he had talked out of going to medical school, charging him with quackery, Freud decided to go public with his anti-medical views. *Die Frage der Laienanalyse* (1926) was the result. He said here what he had said before and would say again: psychoanalysis should not be reduced into a handmaiden of medical psychiatry. It is a vigorous, almost youthful performance; one would not guess from it that Freud was then seventy years old. The little book makes its point energetically, even aggressively, but it does more than this: it serves as an informal popularization of psychoanalytic ideas. The beginner in Freud's thought could do worse than to start with it.

EDITOR'S PREFACE

In the Postscript at the end of this work, Freud himself gives an account of its origin. Stated shortly, it was his reaction to an attempt made by the authorities in 1926 to prevent a prominent non-medical member of the Vienna Psycho-Analytical Society from practising psycho-analysis, on the basis of an old Austrian law against 'quackery. The attempt in fact failed, whether as a result of Freud's intervention or, more probably, owing to the influence of a highly placed official with whom he had discussed the subject. It is this official who was the prototype of the 'Impartial Person' in the pamphlet.

The question at issue, however, was of much more than local importance. Freud himself had long been of the opinion that a medical degree was not an essential need for a practitioner of psycho-analysis and that certain non-medical qualifications *were* essential. This view was and is far from being accepted in every part of the world of psycho-analysis. The American Psycho-analytic Association, for instance, does not admit non-doctors to its 'active membership', whereas the British Psycho-Analytical Society allows them admission provided that they undertake always to work under a doctor's supervision.

The publication of this work of Freud's gave rise to a

sharpening of the argument among psycho-analysts, and the question was ventilated in a long series of reasoned statements (28 in all) by analysts from various countries which were published in 1927 in the two official psycho-analytic periodicals in German and English. The series was brought to an end by Freud himself in the Postscript printed below, in which he replied to his critics and restated his arguments.

This whole discussion may seem to be a parochial one and of no particular interest to the general reader, and, indeed, it is not on its account that this work makes such a wide appeal. It happens, however, that Freud made use of this occasion for giving the very best of his shorter general expositions of psycho-analysis. It is not only clear and comprehensive but entertaining, and its dialogue form affords plenty of scope for the lively irony of Freud's writing. We find in it discussions not only of the deep theoretical basis of psycho-analysis, but also of its therapeutic action and of its technical procedures, as well as of its application in wider psychological fields. The work has, too, the advantage of giving an account of Freud's views in terms belonging to the very latest stage of their development. The Postscript is equally lively, and in it, moreover, Freud gives us some details about the development of his interests during his boyhood and youth which are not to be found elsewhere.

The text of the present translation is derived from Volume XX of *The Standard Edition of the Complete Psychological Works of Sigmund Freud.* (London: The Hogarth Press and the Institute of Psycho-Analysis.)

INTRODUCTION

The title of this small work is not immediately intelligible. I will therefore explain it. 'Layman' = 'Non-doctor'; and the question is whether non-doctors as well as doctors are to be allowed to practise analysis. This question has its limitations both in time and place. In *time*, because up to now no one has been concerned as to *who* practises analysis. Indeed, people have been much too little concerned about it—the one thing they were agreed on was a wish that *no one* should practise it. Various reasons were given for this, but they were based on the same underlying distaste. Thus the demand that only doctors should analyse corresponds to a new and apparently more friendly attitude to analysis—if, that is, it can escape the suspicion of being after all only a slightly modified derivative of the earlier attitude. It is conceded that in some circumstances an analytic treatment shall be undertaken; but, if so, only doctors are to undertake it. The reason for this restriction then becomes a matter for inquiry.

The question is limited in *place* because it does not arise in all countries with equal significance. In Germany and America it would be no more than an academic discussion; for in those countries every patient can have himself treated how and by whom he chooses, and anyone who chooses can, as a 'quack', handle any patients, provided only that he undertakes the responsibility for his actions.[1] The law does not intervene until it is called in to expiate some injury done to the patient. But in Austria, in which and for which I am writing, there is a preventive law, which forbids non-doctors from undertaking the treatment of patients, without waiting for its outcome.[2] So here the question whether laymen (= non-doctors) may treat patients by psycho-analysis has a practical sense. As soon as it is raised, however, it appears to be settled by the wording of the law. Neurotics are patients, laymen are non-doctors, psycho-analysis is a procedure for curing or improving nervous disorders, and all such treatments are reserved to doctors. It follows that laymen are not permitted to practise analysis on neurotics, and are punishable if they nevertheless do so. The position being so simple, one hardly ventures to take up the question of lay analysis. All the same, there are some complications, which the law does not trouble about, but which nevertheless call for consideration. It may perhaps turn out that in this instance the patients are not like other patients, that the laymen are not really laymen, and that the doctors have not exactly the qualities which one has a right to expect of doctors and on which their claims should be based. If this can be proved, there will be justifiable grounds for demanding that the law shall not be applied without modification to the instance before us.

---

[1][This is actually true only of *certain* of the United States. It is also true of Great Britain.]

[2]The same holds good in France.

THE
QUESTION OF
LAY ANALYSIS

I

Whether this happens will depend on people who are not obliged to be familiar with the peculiarities of an analytic treatment. It is our task to give information on the subject to these impartial persons, whom we shall assume to be, at the moment, still in ignorance. It is to be regretted that we cannot let them be present as an audience at a treatment of this kind. But the 'analytic situation' allows the presence of no third person. Moreover the different sessions are of very unequal value. An unauthorized listener who hit upon a chance one of them would as a rule form no useful impression; he would be in danger of not understanding what was passing between the analyst and the patient, or he would be bored. For good or ill, therefore, he must be content with our information, which we shall try to make as trustworthy as possible.

A patient, then, may be suffering from fluctuations in his moods which he cannot control, or from a sense of despondency by which his energy feels paralysed because he thinks he is incapable of doing anything properly, or from a nervous embarrassment among strangers. He may perceive, without understanding the reason for it, that he has difficulties in carrying out his professional work, or indeed any comparatively important decision or any undertaking. He may one

day have suffered from a distressing attack—unknown in its
origin—of feelings of anxiety, and since then have been
unable, without a struggle, to walk along the street alone, or
to travel by train; he may perhaps have had to give up both
entirely. Or, a very remarkable thing, his thoughts may go
their own way and refuse to be directed by his will. They
pursue problems that are quite indifferent to him, but from
which he cannot get free. Quite ludicrous tasks, too, are
imposed on him, such as counting up the windows on the
fronts of houses. And when he has performed simple actions
such as posting a letter or turning off a gas-jet, he finds
himself a moment later doubting whether he has really done
so. This may be no more than an annoyance and a nuisance.
But his state becomes intolerable if he suddenly finds he is
unable to fend off the idea that he has pushed a child under
the wheels of a car or has thrown a stranger off the bridge
into the water, or if he has to ask himself whether he is not
the murderer whom the police are looking for in connexion
with a crime that was discovered that day. It is obvious
nonsense, as he himself knows; he has never done any harm
to anyone; but if he were really the murderer who is being
looked for, his feeling—his sense of guilt—could not be
stronger.

Or again our patient—and this time let us make her a
woman—may suffer in another way and in a different field.
She is a pianist, but her fingers are overcome by cramp and
refuse to serve her. Or when she thinks of going to a party
she promptly becomes aware of a call of nature the satisfaction of which would be incompatible with a social gathering.
She has therefore given up going to parties, dances, theatres,
or concerts. She is overcome by violent headaches or other
painful sensations at times when they are most inconven-
ient. She may even be unable to keep down any meal she
eats—which can become dangerous in the long run. And,

finally, it is a lamentable fact that she cannot tolerate any agitations, which after all are inevitable in life. On such occasions she falls in a faint, often accompanied by muscular spasms that recall sinister pathological states.

Other patients, again, suffer from disturbances in a particular field in which emotional life converges with demands of a bodily sort. If they are men, they find they are incapable of giving physical expression to their tenderest feelings towards the opposite sex, while towards less-loved objects they may perhaps have every reaction at their command. Or their sensual feelings attach them to people whom they despise and from whom they would like to get free; or those same feelings impose requirements on them whose fulfilment they themselves find repulsive. If they are women, they feel prevented by anxiety or disgust or by unknown obstructions from meeting the demands of sexual life; or, if they have surrendered to love, they find themselves cheated of the enjoyment which nature has provided as a reward for such compliance.

All these people recognize that they are ill and go to doctors, by whom people expect nervous disorders like these to be removed. The doctors, too, lay down the categories into which these complaints are divided. They diagnose them, each according to his own standpoint, under different names: neurasthenia, psychasthenia, phobias, obsessional neurosis, hysteria. They examine the organs which produce the symptoms, the heart, the stomach, the bowels, the genitals, and find them healthy. They recommend interruptions in the patient's accustomed mode of life, holidays, strengthening exercises, tonics, and by these means bring about temporary improvements—or no result at all. Eventually the patients hear that there are people who are concerned quite specially with the treatment of such complaints and start an analysis with them.

During this disquisition on the symptoms of neurotics, the Impartial Person, whom I imagine as being present, has been showing signs of impatience. At this point, however, he becomes attentive and interested. 'So now', he says, 'we shall learn what the analyst does with the patient whom the doctor has not been able to help.'

Nothing takes place between them except that they talk to each other. The analyst makes use of no instruments—not even for examining the patient—nor does he prescribe any medicines. If it is at all possible, he even leaves the patient in his environment and in his usual mode of life during the treatment. This is not a necessary condition of course, and may not always be practicable. The analyst agrees upon a fixed regular hour with the patient, gets him to talk, listens to him, talks to him in his turn, and gets him to listen.

The Impartial Person's features now show signs of unmistakable relief and relaxation, but they also clearly betray some contempt. It is as though he were thinking: 'Nothing more than that? Words, words, words, as Prince Hamlet says.' And no doubt he is thinking too of Mephistopheles' mocking speech[1] on how comfortably one can get along with the help of words—lines that no German will ever forget.

'So it is a kind of magic,' he comments: 'you talk, and blow away his ailments.'

Quite true. It *would* be magic if it worked rather quicker. An essential attribute of a magician is speed—one might say suddenness—of success. But analytic treatments take months and even years: magic that is so slow loses its miraculous character. And incidentally do not let us despise the *word*. After all it is a powerful instrument; it is the means

---

[1][In his conversation with the student in *Faust*, Part I, Scene 4.]

by which we convey our feelings to one another, our method of influencing other people. Words can do unspeakable good and cause terrible wounds. No doubt 'in the beginning was the deed'[2] and the word came later; in some circumstances it meant an advance in civilization when deeds were softened into words. But originally the word was magic—a magical act; and it has retained much of its ancient power.

The Impartial Person proceeds: 'Let us suppose that the patient is no better prepared to understand analytic treatment than I am; then how are you going to make him believe in the magic of the word or of the speech that is to free him from his sufferings?'

Some preparation must of course be given to him; and there is a simple way of doing it. We call on him to be completely straightforward with his analyst, to keep nothing back intentionally that comes into his head, and then to put aside *every* reservation that might prevent his reporting certain thoughts or memories. Everyone is aware that there are some things in himself that he would be very unwilling to tell other people or that he considers it altogether out of the question to tell. These are his 'intimacies'. He has a notion too—and this represents a great advance in psychological self-knowledge—that there are other things that one would not care to admit *to oneself:* things that one likes to conceal from oneself and which for that reason one breaks off short and drives out of one's thoughts if, in spite of everything, they turn up. Perhaps he may himself notice that a very remarkable psychological problem begins to appear in this situation—of a thought of his own being kept secret from his own self. It looks as though his own self were no longer the unity which he had always considered it to be, as though there were something else as well in him that could confront

---

[2][*Faust,* Part I, Scene 3.]

that self. He may become obscurely aware of a contrast between a self and a mental life in the wider sense. If now he accepts the demand made by analysis that he shall say everything, he will easily become accessible to an expectation that to have relations and exchanges of thought with someone under such unusual conditions might also lead to peculiar results.

'I understand,' says our Impartial Person. 'You assume that every neurotic has something oppressing him, some secret. And by getting him to tell you about it you relieve his oppression and do him good. That, of course, is the principle of Confession, which the Catholic Church has used from time immemorial in order to make secure its dominance over people's minds.'

We must reply: 'Yes and no!' Confession no doubt plays a part in analysis—as an introduction to it, we might say. But it is very far from constituting the essence of analysis or from explaining its effects. In Confession the sinner tells what he knows; in analysis the neurotic has to tell more. Nor have we heard that Confession has ever developed enough power to get rid of actual pathological symptoms.

'Then, after all, I do not understand,' comes the rejoinder. 'What can you possibly mean by "telling more than he knows"? But I can well believe that as an analyst you gain a stronger influence over your patients than a Father Confessor over his penitents, since your contacts with him are so much longer, more intensive, and also more individual, and since you use this increased influence to divert him from his sick thoughts, to talk him out of his fears, and so on. It would certainly be strange if it were possible by such means to control purely physical phenomena as well, such as vomiting, diarrhoea, convulsions; but I know that influence like that is in fact quite possible if a person is put into a state of hypnosis. By the trouble you take with the patient you

probably succeed in bringing about a hypnotic relation of
that sort with him—a suggestive attachment to yourself—
even though you may not intend to; and in that case the
miraculous results of your treatment are the effect of hypnotic suggestion. But, so far as I know, hypnotic treatment
works much faster than your analysis, which, as you tell me,
lasts for months and years.'

Our Impartial Person cannot be either so ignorant or so
perplexed as we thought to begin with. There are unmistakable signs that he is trying to understand psycho-analysis
with the help of his previous knowledge, that he is trying to
link it up with something he already knows. The difficult
task now lies ahead of us of making it clear to him that he
will not succeed in this: that analysis is a procedure *sui
generis*, something novel and special, which can only be
understood with the help of *new* insights—or hypotheses,
if that sounds better. But he is still waiting for our answer
to his last remarks.

What you say about the special personal influence of the
analyst certainly deserves great attention. An influence of
the kind exists and plays a large part in analysis—but not the
same part as in hypnotism. It ought to be possible to convince you that the situations in the two cases are quite
different. It may be enough to point out that we do not use
this personal influence, the factor of 'suggestion', to suppress
the symptoms of the illness, as happens with *hypnotic* suggestion. Further, it would be a mistake to believe that this
factor is the vehicle and promoter of the treatment throughout its length. At its beginning, no doubt. But later on it
opposes our analytic intentions and forces us to adopt the
most farreaching counter-measures. And I should like to
show by an example how far diverting a patient's thoughts
and talking him out of things are from the technique of
analysis. If a patient of ours is suffering from a sense of guilt,

as though he had committed a serious crime, we do not recommend him to disregard his qualms of conscience and do not emphasize his undoubted innocence; he himself has often tried to do so without success. What we do is to remind him that such a strong and persistent feeling must after all be based on something real, which it may perhaps be possible to discover.

'It would surprise me', comments the Impartial Person, 'if you were able to soothe your patients by agreeing with their sense of guilt in that way. But what *are* your analytic intentions? and what *do* you do with your patients?'

II

If I am to say anything intelligible to you, I shall no doubt have to tell you something of a psychological theory which is not known or not appreciated outside analytic circles. It will be easy to deduce from this theory what we want from our patients and how we obtain it. I shall expound it to you dogmatically, as though it were a complete theoretical structure. But do not suppose that it came into being as such a structure, like a philosophical system. We have developed it very slowly, we have wrestled over every small detail of it, we have unceasingly modified it, keeping a continuous contact with observation, till it has finally taken a shape in which it seems to suffice for our purposes. Only a few years ago I should have had to clothe this theory in other terms. Nor, of course, can I guarantee to you that the form in which it is expressed today will remain the final one. Science, as you know, is not a revelation; long after its beginnings it still lacks the attributes of definiteness, immutability, and infallibility for which human thought so deeply longs. But such as it is, it is all that we can have. If you will further bear in mind that our science is very young, scarcely as old as the century, and that it is concerned with what is perhaps the most difficult material that can be the subject of human research, you will easily be able to adopt the correct attitude towards my exposition. But interrupt me whenever you feel inclined, if you cannot follow me or if you want further explanations.

'I will interrupt you before you have even begun. You say that you intend to expound a new psychology to me; but I should have thought that psychology was no new science. There have been psychologies and psychologists enough; and I heard of great achievements in that field while I was at college.'

I should not dream of disputing them. But if you look into the matter more closely you will have to class these great achievements as belonging rather to the physiology of the sense organs. The theory of mental life could not be developed, because it was inhibited by a single essential misunderstanding. What does it comprise today, as it is taught at college? Apart from those valuable discoveries in the physiology of the senses, a number of classifications and definitions of our mental processes which, thanks to linguistic usage, have become the common property of every educated person. That is clearly not enough to give a view of our mental life. Have you not noticed that every philosopher, every imaginative writer, every historian, and every biographer makes up his own psychology for himself, brings forward his own particular hypotheses concerning the interconnexions and aims of mental acts—all more or less plausible and all equally untrustworthy? There is an evident lack of any common foundation. And it is for that reason too that in the field of psychology there is, so to speak, no respect and no authority. In that field everyone can 'run wild' as he chooses. If you raise a question in physics or chemistry, anyone who knows he possesses no 'technical knowledge' will hold his tongue. But if you venture upon a psychological assertion you must be prepared to meet judgements and contradictions from every quarter. In this field, apparently, there is no 'technical knowledge'. Everyone has a mental life, so everyone regards himself as a psychologist. But that strikes me as an inadequate legal title. The story is told of how someone who applied for a post as a children's nurse was asked if she knew how to look after babies. 'Of course,' she replied, 'why, after all, I was a baby once myself.'

'And you claim that you have discovered this "common foundation" of mental life, which has been overlooked by every psychologist, from observations on *sick people?*'

The source of our findings does not seem to me to deprive them of their value. Embryology, to take an example, would not deserve to be trusted if it could not give a plain explanation of the origin of innate malformations. I have told you of people whose thoughts go their own way, so that they are obliged to worry over problems to which they are perfectly indifferent. Do you think that academic psychology could ever make the smallest contribution towards explaining an abnormality such as that? And, after all, we all of us have the experience at night-time of our thoughts going their own way and creating things which we do not understand, which puzzle us, and which are suspiciously reminiscent of pathological products. Our dreams, I mean. The common people have always firmly believed that dreams have a sense and a value—that they mean something. Academic psychology has never been able to inform us what this meaning is. It could make nothing of dreams. If it attempted to produce explanations, they were non-psychological—such as tracing them to sensory stimuli, or to an unequal depth of sleep in different portions of the brain, and so on. But it is fair to say that a psychology which cannot explain dreams is also useless for an understanding of normal mental life, that it has no claim to be called a science.

'You are becoming aggressive; so you have evidently got on to a sensitive spot. I have heard, it is true, that in analysis great value is attached to dreams, that they are interpreted, and that memories of real events are looked for behind them, and so on. But I have heard as well that the interpretation of dreams is left to the caprice of analysts, and that they themselves have never ceased disputing over the way of interpreting dreams and the justification for drawing conclusions from them. If that is so, you ought not to underline so heavily the advantage that analysis has won over academic psychology.'

There is really a great deal of truth in what you say. It is true that the interpretation of dreams has come to have unequalled importance both for the theory and the practice of analysis. If I seem to be aggressive, that is only a way of defending myself. And when I think of all the mischief some analysts have done with the interpretation of dreams I might lose heart and echo the pessimistic pronouncement of our great satirist Nestroy[1] when he says that every step forward is only half as big as it looks at first. But have you ever found that men do anything but confuse and distort what they get hold of? By the help of a little foresight and self-discipline most of the dangers of dream-interpretation can be avoided with certainty. But you will agree that I shall never come to my exposition if we let ourselves be led aside like this.

'Yes. If I understood rightly, you wanted to tell me about the fundamental postulate of the new psychology.'

That was not what I wanted to begin with. My purpose is to let you hear what pictures we have formed of the structure of the mental apparatus in the course of our analytic studies.

'What do you mean by the "mental apparatus"? and what, may I ask, is it constructed of?'

---

[1][Johann Nestroy (1801–62), famous in Vienna as a writer of comedies and farces.]

It will soon be clear what the mental apparatus is; but I must beg you not to ask what material it is constructed of. That is not a subject of psychological interest. Psychology can be as indifferent to it as, for instance, optics can be to the question of whether the walls of a telescope are made of metal or cardboard. We shall leave entirely on one side the *material* line of approach,[2] but not so the *spatial* one. For we picture the unknown apparatus which serves the activities of the mind as being really like an instrument constructed of several parts (which we speak of as 'agencies'), each of which performs a particular function and which have a fixed spatial relation to one another: it being understood that by spatial relation—'in front of' and 'behind', 'superficial' and 'deep'—we merely mean in the first instance a representation of the regular succession of the functions. Have I made myself clear?

'Scarcely. Perhaps I shall understand it later. But, in any case, here is a strange anatomy of the soul—a thing which, after all, no longer exists at all for the scientists.'

What do you expect? It is a hypothesis like so many others in the sciences: the very earliest ones have always been rather rough. 'Open to revision' we can say in such cases. It seems to me unnecessary for me to appeal here to the 'as if' which has become so popular. The value of a 'fiction' of this kind (as the philosopher Vaihinger[3] would call it) depends on how much one can achieve with its help.

But to proceed. Putting ourselves on the footing of everyday knowledge, we recognize in human beings a mental

---

[2][The question of what *material* the mental apparatus is constructed of.]
[3][Hans Vaihinger (1852–1933). His philosophical system was enunciated in *Die Philosophie des Als Ob*, 1911. An English translation by C. K. Ogden appeared in 1924 under the title *The Philosophy of 'As if'*. The work had a considerable vogue in German-speaking countries, especially after the First World War.]

organization which is interpolated between their sensory stimuli and the perception of their somatic needs on the one hand and their motor acts on the other, and which mediates between them for a particular purpose. We call this organization their *'Ich'* ['ego'; literally, 'I']. Now there is nothing new in this. Each one of us makes this assumption without being a philosopher, and some people even in spite of being philosophers. But this does not, in our opinion, exhaust the description of the mental apparatus. Besides this 'I', we recognize another mental region, more extensive, more imposing, and more obscure than the 'I', and this we call the *'Es'* ['id'; literally, 'it']. The relation between the two must be our immediate concern.

You will probably protest at our having chosen simple pronouns to describe our two agencies or provinces instead of giving them orotund Greek names. In psycho-analysis, however, we like to keep in contact with the popular mode of thinking and prefer to make its concepts scientifically serviceable rather than to reject them. There is no merit in this; we are obliged to take this line; for our theories must be understood by our patients, who are often very intelligent, but not always learned. The impersonal 'it' is immediately connected with certain forms of expression used by normal people. 'It shot through me,' people say; 'there was something in me at that moment that was stronger than me.' *'C'était plus fort que moi.'*

In psychology we can only describe things by the help of analogies. There is nothing peculiar in this; it is the case elsewhere as well. But we have constantly to keep changing these analogies, for none of them lasts us long enough. Accordingly, in trying to make the relation between the ego and the id clear, I must ask you to picture the ego as a kind of façade of the id, as a frontage, like an external, cortical, layer of it. We can hold on to this last analogy. We know that cortical layers owe their peculiar characteristics to the modifying influence of the external medium on which they abut. Thus we suppose that the ego is the layer of the mental apparatus (of the id) which has been modified by the influence of the external world (of reality). This will show you how in psycho-analysis we take spatial ways of looking at things seriously. For us the ego is really something superficial and the id something deeper—looked at from outside, of course. The ego lies between reality and the id, which is what is truly mental.

'I will not ask any questions yet as to how all this can be known. But tell me first what you gain from this distinction between an ego and an id? What leads you to make it?'

Your question shows me the right way to proceed. For the important and valuable thing is to know that the ego and the id differ greatly from each other in several respects. The rules governing the course of mental acts are different in the ego and id; the ego pursues different purposes and by other methods. A great deal could be said about this; but perhaps you will be content with a fresh analogy and an example. Think of the difference between 'the front' and 'behind the lines', as things were during the war. We were not surprised then that some things were different at the front from what they were behind the lines, and that many things were permitted behind the lines which had to be forbidden at the front. The determining influence was, of course, the proximity of the enemy; in the case of mental life it is the proximity of the external world. There was a time when 'outside', 'strange', and 'hostile' were identical concepts. And now we come to the example. In the id there are no conflicts; contradictions and antitheses persist side by side in it unconcernedly, and are often adjusted by the formation of compromises. In similar circumstances the ego feels a conflict which must be decided; and the decision lies in one urge being abandoned in favour of the other. The ego is an organization characterized by a very remarkable trend towards unification, towards synthesis. This characteristic is lacking in the id; it is, as we might say, 'all to pieces'; its different urges pursue their own purposes independently and regardless of one another.

'And if such an important mental region "behind the lines" exists, how can you explain its having been overlooked till the time of analysis?'

That brings us back to one of your earlier questions [p. 14]. Psychology had barred its own access to the region of the id by insisting on a postulate which is plausible enough but untenable: namely, that all mental acts are conscious[4] to us—that being conscious is the criterion of what is mental, and that, if there are processes in our brain which are not conscious, they do not deserve to be called mental acts and are no concern of psychology.

'But I should have thought that was obvious.'

Yes, and that is what psychologists think. Nevertheless it can easily be shown to be false—that is, to be a quite inexpedient distinction. The idlest self-observation shows that ideas may occur to us which cannot have come about without preparation. But you experience nothing of these preliminaries of your thought, though they too must certainly have been of a mental nature; all that enters your consciousness is the ready-made result. Occasionally you can make these preparatory thought-structures conscious *in retrospect,* as though in a reconstruction.

'Probably one's attention was distracted, so that one failed to notice the preparations.'

---

[4][It should be remarked that the German word for 'conscious'—*bewusst*— has a passive form and is regularly used by Freud in a passive sense. Thus he would not as a rule speak of a person being conscious of a sensation but of a sensation being conscious to a person.]

Evasions! You cannot in that way get around the fact that acts of a mental nature, and often very complicated ones, can take place in you, of which your consciousness learns nothing and of which you know nothing. Or are you prepared to suppose that a greater or smaller amount of your 'attention' is enough to transform a non-mental act into a mental one? But what is the use of disputing? There are hypnotic experiments in which the existence of such non-conscious thoughts are irrefutably demonstrated to anyone who cares to learn.

'I shall not retract; but I believe I understand you at last. What you call "ego" is consciousness; and your "id" is the so-called subconscious that people talk about so much nowadays. But why the masquerading with the new names?'

It is not masquerading. The other names are of no use. And do not try to give me literature instead of science. If someone talks of subconsciousness, I cannot tell whether he means the term topographically—to indicate something lying in the mind beneath consciousness—or qualitatively—to indicate another consciousness, a subterranean one, as it were. He is probably not clear about any of it. The only trustworthy antithesis is between conscious and unconscious. But it would be a serious mistake to think that this antithesis coincides with the distinction between ego and id. Of course it would be delightful if it were as simple as that: our theory would have a smooth passage. But things are not so simple. All that is true is that everything that happens in the id is and remains unconscious, and that processes in the ego, and they alone, *can* become conscious. But not all of them are, nor always, nor necessarily; and large portions of the ego can remain permanently unconscious.

The becoming conscious of a mental process is a complicated affair. I cannot resist telling you—once again, dogmatically—our hypotheses about it. The ego, as you will remember, is the external, peripheral layer of the id. Now, we believe that on the outermost surface of this ego there is a special agency directed immediately to the external world, a system, an organ, through the excitation of which alone the phenomenon that we call consciousness comes about. This organ can be equally well excited from outside— thus receiving (with the help of the sense-organs) the stimuli from the external world—and from inside—thus becoming aware, first, of the sensations in the id, and then also of the processes in the ego.

'This is getting worse and worse and I can understand it less and less. After all, what you invited me to was a discussion of the question whether laymen (= non-doctors) ought to undertake analytic treatments. What is the point, then, of all these disquisitions on daring and obscure theories which you cannot convince me are justified?'

I know I cannot convince you. That is beyond any possibility and for that reason beyond my purpose. When we give our pupils theoretical instruction in psycho-analysis, we can see how little impression we are making on them to begin with. They take in the theories of analysis as coolly as other abstractions with which they are nourished. A few of them may perhaps *wish* to be convinced, but there is not a trace of their being so. But we also require that everyone who wants to practise analysis on other people shall first himself submit to an analysis. It is only in the course of this 'self-analysis' (as it is misleadingly termed),[5] when they actually experience as affecting their own person—or rather, their own mind—the processes asserted by analysis, that they acquire the convictions by which they are later guided as analysts. How then could I expect to convince you, the Impartial Person, of the correctness of our theories, when I

---

[5] [This is now usually described as a 'training analysis'.]

can only put before you an abbreviated and therefore unintelligible account of them, without confirming them from your own experiences?

I am acting with a different purpose. The question at issue between us is not in the least whether analysis is sensible or nonsensical, whether it is right in its hypotheses or has fallen into gross errors. I am unrolling our theories before you since that is the best way of making clear to you what the range of ideas is that analysis embraces, on the basis of what hypotheses it approaches a patient and what it does with him. In this way a quite definite light will be thrown on the question of lay analysis. And do not be alarmed. If you have followed me so far you have got over the worst. Everything that follows will be easier for you. But now, with your leave, I will pause to take breath.

III

'I expect you will want to tell me how, on the basis of the theories of psycho-analysis, the origin of a neurotic illness can be pictured.'

I will try to. But for that purpose we must study our ego and our id from a fresh angle, from the *dynamic* one—that is to say, having regard to the forces at work in them and between them. Hitherto we have been content with a *description* of the mental apparatus.

'My only fear is that it may become unintelligible again!'

I hope not. You will soon find your way about in it. Well then, we assume that the forces which drive the mental apparatus into activity are produced in the bodily organs as an expression of the major somatic needs. You will recollect the words of our poet philosopher: 'Hunger and love [are what moves the world].'[1] Incidentally, quite a formidable pair of forces! We give these bodily needs, in so far as they represent an instigation to mental activity, the name of '*Triebe*' [instincts], a word for which we are envied by many modern languages.[2] Well, these instincts fill the id: all the

---

[1][Schiller, 'Die Weltweisen'.]

[2][Various translations have been adopted for the word *Trieb*, the most literal being 'drive'.]

energy in the id, as we may put it briefly, originates from them. Nor have the forces in the ego any other origin; they are derived from those in the id. What, then, do these instincts want? Satisfaction—that is, the establishment of situations in which the bodily needs can be extinguished. A lowering of the tension of need is felt by our organ of consciousness as pleasurable; an increase of it is soon felt as unpleasure. From these oscillations arises the series of feelings of pleasure-unpleasure, in accordance with which the whole mental apparatus regulates its activity. In this connexion we speak of a 'dominance of the pleasure principle'.

If the id's instinctual demands meet with no satisfaction, intolerable conditions arise. Experience soon shows that these situations of satisfaction can only be established with the help of the external world. At that point the portion of the id which is directed towards the external world—the ego—begins to function. If all the driving force that sets the vehicle in motion is derived from the id, the ego, as it were, undertakes the steering, without which no goal can be reached. The instincts in the id press for immediate satisfaction at all costs, and in that way they achieve nothing or even bring about appreciable damage. It is the task of the ego to guard against such mishaps, to mediate between the claims of the id and the objections of the external world. It carries on its activity in two directions. On the one hand, it observes the external world with the help of its sense-organ, the system of consciousness, so as to catch the favourable moment for harmless satisfaction; and on the other hand it influences the id, bridles its 'passions', induces its instincts to postpone their satisfaction and, indeed, if the necessity is recognized, to modify its aims, or, in return for some compensation, to give them up. In so far as it tames the id's impulses in this way, it replaces the pleasure principle, which was formerly alone decisive, by what is known as the 'reality principle', which, though it pursues the same ultimate aims, takes into account the conditions imposed by the real external world. Later, the ego learns that there is yet another way of securing satisfaction besides the *adaptation* to the external world which I have described. It is also possible to intervene in the external world by *changing* it, and to establish in it intentionally the conditions which make satisfaction possible. This activity then becomes the ego's highest function; decisions as to when it is more expedient to control one's passions and bow before reality, and when it is more expedient to side with them and to take arms against the external world—such decisions make up the whole essence of worldly wisdom.

'And does the id put up with being dominated like this by the ego, in spite of being, if I understand you aright, the stronger party?'

Yes, all will be well if the ego is in possession of its whole organization and efficiency, if it has access to all parts of the id and can exercise its influence on them. For there is no natural opposition between ego and id; they belong together, and under healthy conditions cannot in practice be distinguished from each other.

'That sounds very pretty; but I cannot see how in such an ideal relation there can be the smallest room for a pathological disturbance.'

You are right. So long as the ego and its relations to the id fulfil these ideal conditions, there will be no neurotic disturbance. The point at which the illness makes its breach is an unexpected one, though no one acquainted with general pathology will be surprised to find a confirmation of the principle that it is precisely the most important developments and differentiations that carry in them the seeds of illness, of failure of function.

'You are becoming too learned. I cannot follow you.'

I must go back a little bit further. A small living organism is a truly miserable, powerless thing, is it not? compared with the immensely powerful external world, full as it is of destructive influences. A primitive organism, which has not developed any adequate ego-organization, is at the mercy of all these 'traumas'. It lives by the 'blind' satisfaction of its instinctual wishes and often perishes in consequence. The differentiation of an ego is above all a step towards self-preservation. Nothing, it is true, can be learnt from being destroyed; but if one has luckily survived a trauma one takes notice of the approach of similar situations and signalizes the danger by an abbreviated repetition of the impressions one has experienced in connexion with the trauma—by an *affect of anxiety*. This reaction to the perception of the danger now introduces an attempt at flight, which can have a life-saving effect till one has grown strong enough to meet the dangers of the external world in a more active fashion—even aggressively, perhaps.

'All this is very far away from what you promised to tell me.'

You have no notion how close I am to fulfilling my promise. Even in organisms which later develop an efficient ego-organization, their ego is feeble and little differentiated from their id to begin with, during their first years of childhood. Imagine now what will happen if this powerless ego experiences an instinctual demand from the id which it would already like to resist (because it senses that to satisfy it is dangerous and would conjure up a traumatic situation, a collision with the external world) but which it cannot control, because it does not yet possess enough strength to do so. In such a case the ego treats the instinctual danger as if it was an external one; it makes an attempt at flight, draws back from this portion of the id, and leaves it to its fate, after withholding from it all the contributions which it usually makes to instinctual impulses. The ego, as we put it, institutes a *repression* of these instinctual impulses. For the moment this has the effect of fending off the danger; but one cannot confuse the inside and the outside with impunity. One cannot run away from oneself. In repression the ego is following the pleasure principle, which it is usually in the habit of correcting; and it is bound to suffer damage in revenge. This lies in the ego's having permanently narrowed its sphere of influence. The repressed instinctual impulse is now isolated, left to itself, inaccessible, but also uninfluenceable. It goes its own way. Even later, as a rule, when the ego has grown stronger, it still cannot lift the repression; its synthesis is impaired, a part of the id remains forbidden ground to the ego. Nor does the isolated instinctual impulse remain idle; it understands how to make up for being denied normal satisfaction; it produces psychical derivatives which take its place; it links itself to other processes which by its influence it likewise tears away from the ego; and finally it breaks through into the ego and into consciousness in the form of an unrecognizably distorted substitute, and creates what we call a symptom. All at once the nature of a neurotic disorder becomes clear to us: on the one hand an ego which is inhibited in its synthesis, which has no influence on parts of the id, which must renounce some of its activities in order to avoid a fresh collision with what has been repressed, and which exhausts itself in what are for the most part vain acts of defence against the symptoms, the derivatives of the repressed impulses; and on the other hand an id in which individual instincts have made themselves independent, pursue their aims regardless of the interests of the person as a whole, and henceforth obey the laws only of the primitive psychology that rules in the depths of the id. If we survey the whole situation we arrive at a simple formula for the origin of a neurosis: the ego has made an attempt to suppress certain portions of the id *in an inappropriate manner*, this attempt has failed, and the id has taken its revenge. A neurosis is thus the result of a conflict between the ego and the id, upon which the ego has embarked because, as careful investigation shows, it wishes at all costs to retain its adaptability in relation to the real external world. The disagreement is between the external world and the id; and it is because the ego, loyal to its inmost nature, takes sides with the external world that it becomes involved in a conflict with its id. But please observe that what creates the determinant for the illness is not the fact of this conflict—for disagreements of this kind between reality and the id are unavoidable and it is one of the ego's standing tasks to mediate in them—but the circumstance that the ego has made use of the inefficient instrument of repression for dealing with the conflict. But this in turn is due to the fact that the ego, at the time at which it was set the task, was undeveloped and powerless. The decisive repressions all take place in early childhood.

'What a remarkable business! I shall follow your advice and not make criticisms, since you only want to show me what psycho-analysis believes about the origin of neurosis so that you can go on to say how it sets about combating it. I should have various questions to ask and later on I shall raise some of them. But at the moment I myself feel tempted for once to carry your train of thought further and to venture upon a theory of my own. You have expounded the relation between external world, ego, and id, and you have laid it down as the determinant of a neurosis that the ego in its dependence on the external world struggles against the id. Is not the opposite case conceivable of the ego in a conflict of this kind allowing itself to be dragged away by the id and disavowing its regard for the external world? What happens in a case like that? From my lay notions of the nature of insanity I should say that such a decision on the part of the ego might be the determinant of insanity. After all, a turning away of that kind from reality seems to be the essence of insanity.'

Yes. I myself have thought of that possibility, and indeed I believe it meets the facts—though to prove the suspicion true would call for a discussion of some highly complicated considerations. Neuroses and psychoses are evidently intimately related, but they must nevertheless differ in some decisive respect. That might well be the side taken by the ego in a conflict of this kind. In both cases the id would retain its characteristic of blind inflexibility.

'Well, go on! What hints on the treatment of neurotic illnesses does your theory give?'

It is easy now to describe our therapeutic aim. We try to restore the ego, to free it from its restrictions, and to give it back the command over the id which it has lost owing to its early repressions. It is for this one purpose that we carry out analysis, our whole technique is directed to this aim. We have to seek out the repressions which have been set up and to urge the ego to correct them with our help and to deal with conflicts better than by an attempt at flight. Since these repressions belong to the very early years of childhood, the work of analysis leads us, too, back to that period. Our path to these situations of conflict, which have for the most part been forgotten and which we try to revive in the patient's memory, is pointed out to us by his symptoms, dreams, and free associations. These must, however, first be interpreted—translated—for, under the influence of the psychology of the id, they have assumed forms of expression that are strange to our comprehension. We may assume that whatever associations, thoughts, and memories the patient is unable to communicate to us without internal struggles are in some way connected with the repressed material or are its derivatives. By encouraging the patient to disregard his resistances to telling us these things, we are educating his ego to overcome its inclination towards attempts at flight and to tolerate an approach to what is repressed. In the end, if the situation of the repression can be successfully reproduced in his memory, his compliance will be brilliantly rewarded. The whole difference between his age then and now works in his favour; and the thing from which his childish ego fled in terror will often seem to his adult and strengthened ego no more than child's play.

IV

'Everything you have told me so far has been psychology. It has often sounded strange, difficult, or obscure; but it has always been—if I may put it so—"pure." I have known very little hitherto, no doubt, about your psycho-analysis; but the rumour has nevertheless reached my ears that you are principally occupied with things that have no claim to that predicate. The fact that you have not yet touched on anything of the kind makes me feel that you are deliberately keeping something back. And there is another doubt that I cannot suppress. After all, as you yourself say, neuroses are disturbances of mental life. Is it possible, then, that such important things as our ethics, our conscience, our ideals, play no part at all in these profound disturbances?'

So you feel that a consideration both of what is lowest and of what is highest has been missing from our discussions up till now? The reason for that is that we have not yet considered the *contents* of mental life at all. But allow me now for once myself to play the part of an interrupter who holds up the progress of the conversation. I have talked so much psychology to you because I wanted you to get the impression that the work of analysis is a part of applied psychology—and, moreover, of a psychology that is unknown outside analysis. An analyst must therefore first and foremost have learnt this psychology, this depth-psychology or psychology of the unconscious, or as much of it at least as is known today. We shall need this as a basis for our later conclusions. But now, what was it you meant by your allusion to 'purity'?

'Well, it is generally reported that in analyses the most intimate—and the nastiest—events in sexual life come up for discussion in every detail. If that is so—I have not been able to gather from your psychological discussions that it is necessarily so—it would be a strong argument in favour of restricting these treatments to doctors. How could one dream of allowing such dangerous liberties to people of whose discretion one was not sure and of whose character one had no guarantee?'

It is true that doctors enjoy certain privileges in the sphere of sex: they are even allowed to inspect people's genitals—though they were not allowed to in the East and though some idealistic reformers (you know whom I have in mind)[1] have disputed this privilege. But you want to know in the first place whether it is so in analysis and why it must be so. Yes, it is so.

And it must be so, firstly because analysis is entirely founded on complete candour. Financial circumstances, for instance, are discussed with equal detail and openness: things are said that are kept back from every fellow-citizen, even if he is not a competitor or a tax-collector. I will not dispute—indeed, I will myself insist with energy—that this obligation to candour puts a grave moral responsibility on the analyst as well. And it must be so, secondly, because factors from sexual life play an extremely important, a dominating, perhaps even a *specific*, part among the causes and precipitating factors of neurotic illnesses. What else can

---

[1][No doubt Tolstoy and his followers.]

analysis do but keep close to its subject-matter, to the material brought up by the patient? The analyst never entices his patient on to the ground of sex. He does not say to him in advance: 'We shall be dealing with the intimacies of your sexual life!' He allows him to begin what he has to say wherever he pleases, and quietly waits until the patient himself touches on sexual things. I used always to warn my pupils: 'Our opponents have told us that we shall come upon cases in which the factor of sex plays no part. Let us be careful not to introduce it into our analyses and so spoil our chance of finding such a case.' But so far none of us has had that good fortune.

I am aware, of course, that our recognition of sexuality has become—whether admittedly or not—the strongest motive for other people's hostility to analysis. Can that shake our confidence? It merely shows us how neurotic our whole civilized life is, since ostensibly normal people do not behave very differently from neurotics. At a time when psycho-analysis was solemnly put on its trial before the learned societies of Germany—today things have grown altogether quieter—one of the speakers claimed to possess peculiar authority because, so he said, he even allowed his patients to talk: for diagnostic purposes, clearly, and to test the assertions of analysts. 'But,' he added, 'if they begin to talk about sexual matters I shut their mouths.' What do you think of that as a method of demonstration? The learned society applauded the speaker to the echo instead of feeling suitably ashamed on his account. Only the triumphant certainty afforded by the consciousness of prejudices held in common can explain this speaker's want of logical thought. Years later a few of those who had at that time been my followers gave in to the need to free human society from the yoke of sexuality which psycho-analysis was seeking to impose on it. One of them explained that what is sexual does not mean sexuality at all, but something else, something abstract and mystical. And another actually declared that sexual life is merely one of the spheres in which human beings seek to put in action their driving need for power and domination. They have met with much applause, for the moment at least.

'I shall venture, for once in a way, to take sides on that point. It strikes me as extremely bold to assert that sexuality is not a natural, primitive need of living organisms, but an expression of something else. One need only take the example of animals.'

That makes no difference. There is no mixture, however absurd, that society will not willingly swallow down if it is advertised as an antidote to the dreaded predominance of sexuality.

I confess, moreover, that the dislike that you yourself have betrayed of assigning to the factor of sexuality so great a part in the causation of neurosis—I confess that this scarcely seems to me consistent with your task as an Impartial Person. Are you not afraid that this antipathy may interfere with your passing judgement?

'I'm sorry to hear you say that. Your reliance on me seems to be shaken. But in that case why not have chosen someone else as your Impartial Person?'

Because that someone else would not have thought any differently from you. But if he had been prepared from the first to recognize the importance of sexual life, everyone would have exclaimed: 'Why, that is no Impartial Person, he is one of your supporters!' No, I am far from abandoning the expectation of being able to influence your opinions. I must admit, however, that from my point of view this situation is different from the one we dealt with earlier. As regards our psychological discussions it is a matter of indifference to me whether you believe me or not, provided only that you get an impression that what we are concerned with are purely psychological problems. But here, as regards the question of sexuality, I should nevertheless be glad if you were accessible to the realization that your strongest motive for contradiction is precisely the ingrained hostility which you share with so many other people.

'But after all I am without the experience that has given you your unshakeable certainty.'

Very well. I can now proceed with my exposition. Sexual life is not simply something spicy; it is also a serious scientific problem. There was much that was novel to be learnt about it, many strange things to be explained. I told you just now that analysis has to go back into the early years of the patient's childhood, because the decisive repressions have taken place then, while his ego was feeble. But surely in childhood there is no sexual life? surely it only starts at puberty? On the contrary. We have to learn that sexual instinctual impulses accompany life from birth onwards, and that it is precisely in order to fend off those instincts that the infantile ego institutes repressions. A remarkable coincidence, is it not? that small children should already be struggling against the power of sexuality, just as the speaker in the learned society was to do later, and later still my followers who have set up their own theories. How does that come about? The most general explanation would be that our civilization is built up entirely at the expense of sexuality; but there is much more to be said on the subject.

The discovery of infantile sexuality is one of those of which we have reason to feel ashamed [because of its obviousness]. A few paediatricians have, it seems, always known about it, and a few children's nurses. Clever men, who call themselves child psychologists, have thereupon spoken in tones of reproach of a 'desecration of the innocence of childhood'. Once again, sentiment instead of argument!

Events of that kind are of daily occurrence in political bodies. A member of the Opposition rises and denounces some piece of maladministration in the Civil Service, in the Army, in the Judiciary, and so on. Upon this another member, preferably one of the Government, declares that such statements are an affront to the sense of honour of the body politic, of the army, of the dynasty, or even of the nation. So they are as good as untrue. Feelings such as these can tolerate no affronts.

The sexual life of children is of course different from that of adults. The sexual function, from its beginnings to the definitive form in which it is so familiar to us, undergoes a complicated process of development. It grows together from numerous component instincts with different aims and passes through several phases of organization till at last it comes into the service of reproduction. Not all the component instincts are equally serviceable for the final outcome; they must be diverted, remodelled, and in part suppressed. Such a far-reaching course of development is not always passed through without a flaw; inhibitions in development take place, partial fixations at early stages of development. If obstacles arise later on to the exercise of the sexual function, the sexual urge—the libido, as we call it—is apt to hark back to these earlier points of fixation. The study of the sexuality of children and its transformations up to maturity has also given us the key to an understanding of what are known as the sexual perversions, which people used always to describe with all the requisite indications of disgust but whose origin they were never able to explain. The whole topic is of uncommon interest, but for the purposes of our conversation there is not much sense in telling you more about it. To find one's way about in it one of course needs anatomical and physiological knowledge, all of which is unfortunately not to be acquired in medical schools. But a familiarity with the history of civilization and with mythology is equally indispensable.

'After all that, I still cannot form any picture of the sexual life of children.'

Then I will pursue the subject further; in any case it is not easy for me to get away from it. I will tell you, then, that the most remarkable thing about the sexual life of children seems to me that it passes through the whole of its very far-reaching development in the first five years of life. From then onwards until puberty there stretches what is known as the period of latency. During it sexuality normally advances no further; on the contrary, the sexual urges diminish in strength and many things are given up and forgotten which the child did and knew. During that period of life, after the early efflorescence of sexuality has withered, such attitudes of the ego as shame, disgust, and morality arise, which are destined to stand up against the later tempest of puberty and to lay down the path of the freshly awakening sexual desires. This 'diphasic onset',[2] as it is named, of sexual life has a great deal to do with the genesis of neurotic illnesses. It seems to occur only in human beings, and it is perhaps one of the determinants of the human privilege of becoming neurotic. The prehistory of sexual life was just as much overlooked before psycho-analysis as, in another department, the background to conscious mental life. You will rightly suspect that the two are intimately connected.

There is much to be told, for which our expectations have not prepared us, about the contents, manifestations, and achievements of this early period of sexuality. For instance, you will no doubt be surprised to hear how often little boys are afraid of being eaten up by their father. (And you may also be surprised at my including this fear among the phe-

---

[2] [Onset in two waves.]

nomena of sexual life.) But I may remind you of the mytho-
logical tale which you may still recall from your schooldays
of how the god Kronos swallowed his children. How strange
this must have sounded to you when you first heard it! But
I suppose none of us thought about it at the time. Today we
can also call to mind a number of fairy tales in which some
ravenous animal like a wolf appears, and we shall recognize
it as a disguise of the father. And this is an opportunity of
assuring you that it was only through the knowledge of
infantile sexuality that it became possible to understand
mythology and the world of fairy tales. Here then something
has been gained as a by-product of analytic studies.

You will be no less surprised to hear that male children
suffer from a fear of being robbed of their sexual organ by
their father, so that this fear of being castrated has a most
powerful influence on the development of their character
and in deciding the direction to be followed by their sexuality. And here again mythology may give you the courage to
believe psycho-analysis. The same Kronos who swallowed his
children also emasculated his father Uranus, and was afterwards himself emasculated in revenge by his son Zeus, who
had been rescued through his mother's cunning. If you have
felt inclined to suppose that all that psycho-analysis reports
about the early sexuality of children is derived from the
disordered imagination of the analysts, you must at least
admit that their imagination has created the same product
as the imaginative activities of primitive man, of which
myths and fairy tales are the precipitate. The alternative
friendlier, and probably also the more pertinent, view would
be that in the mental life of children today we can still
detect the same archaic factors which were once dominant
generally in the primeval days of human civilization. In his
mental development the child would be repeating the history of his race in an abbreviated form, just as embryology

long since recognized was the case with somatic development.

Another characteristic of early infantile sexuality is that the female sexual organ proper as yet plays no part in it: the child has not yet discovered it. Stress falls entirely on the male organ, all the child's interest is directed towards the question of whether it is present or not. We know less about the sexual life of little girls than of boys. But we need not feel ashamed of this distinction; after all, the sexual life of adult women is a 'dark continent' for psychology. But we have learnt that girls feel deeply their lack of a sexual organ that is equal in value to the male one; they regard themselves on that account as inferior, and this 'envy for the penis' is the origin of a whole number of characteristic feminine reactions.

It is also characteristic of children that their two excretory needs are cathected [charged] with sexual interest. Later on, education draws a sharp distinction here, which is once more obliterated in the practice of joking. It may seem to us an unsavoury fact, but it takes quite a long time for children to develop feelings of disgust. This is not disputed even by people who insist otherwise on the seraphic purity of the child's mind.

Nothing, however, deserves more notice than the fact that children regularly direct their sexual wishes towards their nearest relatives—in the first place, therefore, towards their father and mother, and afterwards towards their brothers and sisters. The first object of a boy's love is his mother, and of a girl's her father (except in so far as an innate bisexual disposition favours the simultaneous presence of the contrary attitude). The other parent is felt as a disturbing rival and not infrequently viewed with strong hostility. You must understand me aright. What I mean to say is not that the child wants to be treated by its favourite parent merely with the kind of affection which we adults like to regard as the essence of the parent-child relation. No, analysis leaves us in no doubt that the child's wishes extend beyond such affection to all that we understand by sensual satisfaction— so far, that is, as the child's powers of imagination allow. It is easy to see that the child never guesses the actual facts of sexual intercourse; he replaces them by other notions derived from his own experience and feelings. As a rule his wishes culminate in the intention to bear, or in some indefinable way to procreate, a baby. Boys, too, in their ignorance, do not exclude themselves from the wish to bear a baby. We give the whole of this mental structure the name of 'Oedipus complex', after the familiar Greek legend. With the end of the early sexual period it should normally be given up, should radically disintegrate and become transformed; and the products of this transformation are destined for important functions in later mental life. But as a rule this is not effected radically enough, in which case puberty brings about a revival of the complex, which may have serious consequences.

I am surprised that you are still silent. That can scarcely mean consent. In asserting that a child's first choice of an object is, to use the technical term, an incestuous one, analysis no doubt once more hurt the most sacred feelings of humanity, and might well be prepared for a corresponding amount of disbelief, contradiction, and attack. And these it has received in abundance. Nothing has damaged it more in the good opinion of its contemporaries than its hypothesis of the Oedipus complex as a structure universally bound to human destiny. The Greek myth, incidentally, must have had the same meaning; but the majority of men today, learned and unlearned alike, prefer to believe that Nature has laid down an innate abhorrence in us as a guard against the possibility of incest.

But let us first summon history to our aid. When Caius Julius Caesar landed in Egypt, he found the young Queen Cleopatra (who was soon to become so important to him) married to her still younger brother Ptolemy. In an Egyptian dynasty there was nothing peculiar in this; the Ptolemies, who were of Greek origin, had merely carried on the custom which had been practised by their predecessors, the ancient Pharaohs, for a few thousand years. This, however, was merely brother-and-sister incest, which even at the present time is not judged so harshly. So let us turn to our chief witness in matters concerning primeval times—mythology. It informs us that the myths of every people, and not only of the Greeks, are filled with examples of love-affairs between fathers and daughters and even between mothers and sons. Cosmology, no less than the genealogy of royal races, is founded upon incest. For what purpose do you suppose these legends were created? To brand gods and kings as criminals? to fasten on them the abhorrence of the human race? Rather, surely, because incestuous wishes are a primordial human heritage and have never been fully overcome, so that their fulfilment was still granted to gods and their descendants when the majority of common humans were already obliged to renounce them. It is in complete harmony with these lessons of history and mythology that we find incestuous wishes still present and operative in the childhood of the individual.

'I might take it amiss that you tried to keep back all this about infantile sexuality from me. It seems to me most interesting, particularly on account of its connexion with human pre-history.'

I was afraid it might take us too far from our purpose. But perhaps after all it will be of use.

'Now tell me, though, what certainty can you offer for your analytic findings on the sexual life of children? Is your conviction based solely on points of agreement with mythology and history?'

Oh, by no means. It is based on direct observation. What happened was this. We had begun by inferring the content of sexual childhood from the analysis of adults—that is to say, some twenty or forty years later. Afterwards, we undertook analysis on children themselves, and it was no small triumph when we were thus able to confirm in them everything that we had been able to divine, in spite of the amount to which it had been overlaid and distorted in the interval.

'What? You have had small children in analysis? children of less than six years? *Can* that be done? And is it not most risky for the children?'

It can be done very well. It is hardly to be believed what goes on in a child of four or five years old. Children are very active-minded at that age; their early sexual period is also a period of intellectual flowering. I have an impression that with the onset of the latency period they become mentally inhibited as well, stupider. From that time on, too, many children lose their physical charm. And, as regards the damage done by early analysis, I may inform you that the first child on whom the experiment was ventured, nearly twenty years ago, has since then grown into a healthy and capable young man, who has passed through his puberty irreproachably, in spite of some severe psychical traumas. It may be hoped that things will turn out no worse for the other 'victims' of early analysis. Much that is of interest attaches to these child analyses; it is possible that in the future they will become still more important. From the point of view of theory, their value is beyond question. They give unambiguous information on problems which remain unsolved in the analyses of adults; and they thus protect the analyst from errors that might have momentous consequences for him. One surprises the factors that lead to the formation of a neurosis while they are actually at work and one cannot then mistake them. In the child's interest, it is true, analytic influence must be combined with educational measures. The technique has still to receive its shaping. But practical interest is aroused by the observation that a very large number of our children pass through a plainly neurotic phase in the course of their development. Since we have learnt how to look more sharply, we are tempted to say that neurosis in children is not the exception but the rule, as though it could scarcely be avoided on the path from the innate disposition of infancy to civilized society. In most cases this neurotic phase in childhood is overcome spontaneously. But may it not also regularly leave its traces in the average healthy adult? On the other hand in those who are neurotics in later life we never fail to find links with the illness in childhood, though at the time it need not have been very noticeable. In a precisely analogous way physicians today, I believe, hold the view that each one of us has gone through an attack of tuberculosis in his childhood. It is true that in the case of the neurosis the factor of immunization does not operate, but only the factor of predisposition.

Let me return to your question about certainty. We have become quite generally convinced from the direct analytic examination of children that we were right in our interpretation of what adults told us about their childhood. In a number of cases, however, another sort of confirmation has become possible. The material of the analysis of some patients has enabled us to reconstruct certain external happenings, certain impressive events of their childhood years, of which they have preserved no conscious memory. Lucky accidents, information from parents or nurses, have afterwards provided irrefutable evidence that these occurrences which we had inferred really did take place. This, of course, has not happened often, but when it has it has made an overwhelming impression. The correct reconstruction, you must know, of such forgotten experiences of childhood always has a great therapeutic effect, whether they permit of objective confirmation or not. These events owe their importance, of course, to their having occurred at such an early age, at a time when they could still produce a traumatic effect on the feeble ego.

'And what sort of events can these be, that have to be discovered by analysis?'

Various sorts. In the first place, impressions capable of permanently influencing the child's budding sexual life—such as observations of sexual activities between adults, or sexual experiences of his own with an adult or another child (no rare events); or, again, overhearing conversations, understood either at the time or retrospectively, from which the child thought it could draw conclusions about mysterious or uncanny matters; or again, remarks or actions by the child himself which give evidence of significant attitudes of affection or enmity towards other people. It is of special importance in an analysis to induce a memory of the patient's own forgotten sexual activity as a child and also of the intervention by the adults which brought it to an end.

'That gives me an opportunity to bring up a question that I have long wanted to ask. What, then, is the nature of this "sexual activity" of children at an early age, which, as you say, was overlooked before the days of analysis?'

It is an odd thing that the regular and essential part of this sexual activity was *not* overlooked. Or rather, it is by no means odd; for it was impossible to overlook it. Children's sexual impulses find their main expressions in self-gratification by friction of their own genitals, or, more precisely, of the male portion of them. The extraordinarily wide distribution of this form of childish 'naughtiness' was always known to adults, and it was regarded as a grave sin and severely punished. But please do not ask me how people could reconcile these observations of the immoral inclinations of children—for children do it, as they themselves say, because it gives them pleasure—with the theory of their innate purity and non-sensuality. You must get our opponents to solve this riddle. *We* have a more important problem before us. What attitude should we adopt towards the sexual activity of early childhood? We know the responsibility we are incurring if we suppress it; but we do not venture to let it take its course without restriction. Among races at a low level of civilization, and among the lower strata of civilized races, the sexuality of children seems to be given free rein. This probably provides a powerful protection against the subsequent development of neuroses in the individual. But does it not at the same time involve an extraordinary loss of the aptitude for cultural achievements? There is a good deal to suggest that here we are faced by a new Scylla and Charybdis.

But whether the interests which are stimulated by the study of the sexual life of neurotics create an atmosphere favourable to the encouragement of lasciviousness—*that* is a question which I venture to leave to your own judgement.

V

'I believe I understand your purpose. You want to show me what kind of knowledge is needed in order to practise analysis, so that I may be able to judge whether only doctors should have a right to do so. Well, so far very little to do with medicine has turned up: a great deal of psychology and a little biology or sexual science. But perhaps we have not got to the end?'

Decidedly not. There are still gaps to be filled. May I make a request? Will you describe how you now picture an analytic treatment?—just as though you had to undertake one yourself.

'A fine idea, to be sure! No, I have not the least intention of settling our controversy by an experiment of that sort. But just to oblige, I will do what you ask—the responsibility will be yours. Very well. I will suppose that the patient comes to me and complains of his troubles. I promise him recovery or improvement if he will follow my directions. I call on him to tell me with perfect candour everything that he knows and that occurs to him, and not to be deterred from that intention even if some things are disagreeable to say. Have I taken in the rule properly?'

Yes. You should add: 'even if what occurs to him seems unimportant or senseless.'

'I will add that. Thereupon he begins to talk and I listen. And what then? I infer from what he tells me the kind of impressions, experiences, and wishes which he has repressed because he came across them at a time when his ego was still feeble and was afraid of them instead of dealing with them. When he has learnt this from me, he puts himself back in the old situations and with my help he manages better. The limitations to which his ego was tied then disappear, and he is cured. Is that right?'

Bravo! bravo! I see that once again people will be able to accuse me of having made an analyst of someone who is not a doctor. You have mastered it all admirably.

'I have done no more than repeat what I have heard from you—as though it was something I had learnt by heart. All the same, I cannot form any picture of how I should do it, and I am at quite a loss to understand why a job like that should take an hour a day for so many months. After all, an ordinary person has not as a rule experienced such a lot, and what was repressed in childhood is probably in every case the same.'

When one really practises analysis one learns all kinds of things besides. For instance: you would not find it at all such a simple matter to deduce from what the patient tells you the experiences he has forgotten and the instinctual impulses he has repressed. He says something to you which at first means as little to you as it does to him. You will have to make up your mind to look at the material which he delivers to you in obedience to the rule in a quite special way: as though it were ore, perhaps, from which its content of precious metal has to be extracted by a particular process. You will be prepared, too, to work over many tons of ore which may contain but little of the valuable material you are in search of. Here we should have a first reason for the prolonged character of the treatment.

'But how does one work over this raw material—to keep to your simile?'

By assuming that the patient's remarks and associations are only distortions of what you are looking for—allusions, as it were, from which you have to guess what is hidden behind them. In a word, this material, whether it consists of memories, associations, or dreams, has first to be *interpreted*. You will do this, of course, with an eye to the expectations you have formed as you listened, thanks to your special knowledge.

' "Interpret!" A nasty word! I dislike the sound of it; it robs me of all certainty. If everything depends on my interpretation who can guarantee that I interpret right? So after all everything *is* left to my caprice.'

Just a moment! Things are not quite as bad as that. Why do you choose to except your own mental processes from the rule of law which you recognize in other people's? When you have attained some degree of self-discipline and have certain knowledge at your disposal, your interpretations will be independent of your personal characteristics and will hit the mark. I am not saying that the analyst's·personality is a matter of indifference for this portion of his task. A kind of sharpness of hearing for what is unconscious and repressed, which is not possessed equally by everyone, has a part to play. And here, above all, we are brought to the analyst's obligation to make himself capable, by a deep-going analysis of his own, of the unprejudiced reception of the analytic material. Something, it is true, still remains over: something comparable to the 'personal equation' in astronomical observations. This individual factor will always play a larger part in psycho-analysis than elsewhere. An abnormal person can become an accurate physicist; as an analyst he will be hampered by his own abnormality from seeing the pictures of mental life undistorted. Since it is impossible to demonstrate to anyone his own abnormality, general agreement in matters of depth-psychology will be particularly hard to reach. Some psychologists, indeed, think it is quite impossible and that every fool has an equal right to give out his folly as wisdom. I confess that I am more of an optimist about this. After all, our experiences show that fairly satisfactory agreements can be reached even in psychology. Every field of research has its particular difficulty which we must try to eliminate. And, moreover, even in the interpretative art of analysis there is much that can be learnt like any other material of study: for instance, in connexion with the peculiar method of indirect representation through symbols.

'Well, I no longer have any desire to undertake an analytic treatment even in my imagination. Who can say what other surprises I might meet with?'

You are quite right to give up the notion. You see how much more training and practice would be needed. When you have found the right interpretation, another task lies ahead. You must wait for the right moment at which you can communicate your interpretation to the patient with some prospect of success.

'How can one always tell the right moment?'

That is a question of tact, which can become more refined with experience. You will be making a bad mistake if, in an effort, perhaps, at shortening the analysis, you throw your interpretations at the patient's head as soon as you have found them. In that way you will draw expressions of resistance, rejection, and indignation from him; but you will not enable his ego to master his repressed material. The formula is: to wait till he has come so near to the repressed material that he has only a few more steps to take under the lead of the interpretation you propose.

'I believe I should never learn to do that. And if I carry

out these precautions in making my interpretation, what next?'

It will then be your fate to make a discovery for which you were not prepared.

'And what may that be?'

That you have been deceived in your patient; that you cannot count in the slightest on his collaboration and compliance; that he is ready to place every possible difficulty in the way of your common work—in a word, that he has no wish whatever to be cured.

'Well! that is the craziest thing you have told me yet. And I do not believe it either. The patient who is suffering so much, who complains so movingly about his troubles, who is making so great a sacrifice for the treatment—you say he has no wish to be cured! But of course you do not mean what you say.'

Calm yourself! I *do* mean it. What I said was the truth—not the whole truth, no doubt, but a very noteworthy part of it. The patient wants to be cured—but he also wants not to be. His ego has lost its unity, and for that reason his will has no unity either. If that were not so, he would be no neurotic.

' "Were I sagacious, I should not be Tell!" '[1]

The derivatives of what is repressed have broken into his ego and established themselves there; and the ego has as little control over trends from that source as it has over what is actually repressed, and as a rule it knows nothing about them. These patients, indeed, are of a peculiar nature and raise difficulties with which we are not accustomed to reckon. All our social institutions are framed for people with a united and normal ego, which one can classify as good or

---

[1][Schiller, *Wilhelm Tell*, Act III, Scene 3.]

bad, which either fulfils its function or is altogether eliminated by an overpowering influence. Hence the juridical alternative: responsible or irresponsible. None of these distinctions apply to neurotics. It must be admitted that there is difficulty in adapting social demands to their psychological condition. This was experienced on a large scale during the last war. Were the neurotics who evaded service malingerers or not? They were both. If they were treated as malingerers and if their illness was made highly uncomfortable, they recovered; if after being ostensibly restored they were sent back into service, they promptly took flight once more into illness. Nothing could be done with them. And the same is true of neurotics in civil life. They complain of their illness but exploit it with all their strength; and if someone tries to take it away from them they defend it like the proverbial lioness with her young. Yet there would be no sense in reproaching them for this contradiction.

'But would not the best plan be not to give these difficult people any treatment at all, but to leave them to themselves? I cannot think it is worth while to expend such great efforts over each of them as you lead me to suppose that you make.'

I cannot approve of your suggestion. It is undoubtedly a more proper line to accept the complications of life rather than struggle against them. It may be true that not every neurotic whom we treat is worth the expenditure of an analysis; but there are some very valuable individuals among them as well. We must set ourselves the goal of bringing it about that as few human beings as possible enter civilized life with such a defective mental equipment. And for that purpose we must collect much experience and learn to understand many things. Every analysis can be instructive and bring us a yield of new understanding quite apart from the personal value of the individual patient.

'But if a volitional impulse has been formed in the patient's ego which wishes to retain the illness, it too must have its reasons and motives and be able in some ways to justify itself. But it is impossible to see why anyone should want to be ill or what he can get out of it.'

Oh, that is not so hard to understand. Think of the war neurotics, who do not have to serve, precisely because they are ill. In civil life illness can be used as a screen to gloss over incompetence in one's profession or in competition with other people; while in the family it can serve as a means for sacrificing the other members and extorting proofs of their love or for imposing one's will upon them. All of this lies fairly near the surface; we sum it up in the term 'gain from illness'. It is curious, however, that the patient—that is, his ego—nevertheless knows nothing of the whole concatenation of these motives and the actions which they involve. One combats the influence of these trends by compelling the ego to take cognizance of them. But there are other motives, that lie still deeper, for holding on to being ill, which are not so easily dealt with. But these cannot be understood without a fresh journey into psychological theory.

'Please go on. A little more theory will make no odds now.'

When I described the relation between the ego and the id to you, I suppressed an important part of the theory of the mental apparatus. For we have been obliged to assume that within the ego itself a particular agency has become differentiated, which we name the super-ego. This super-ego occupies a special position between the ego and the id. It belongs to the ego and shares its high degree of psychological organization; but it has a particularly intimate connexion with the id. It is in fact a precipitate of the first object-cathexes of the id and is the heir to the Oedipus complex after its demise.[2] This super-ego can confront the ego and treat it like an object; and it often treats it very harshly. It is as important for the ego to remain on good terms with the super-ego as with the id. Estrangements between the ego and the super-ego are of great significance in mental life. You will already have guessed that the super-ego is the vehicle of the phenomenon that we call conscience. Mental health very much depends on the super-ego's being normally developed—that is, on its having become sufficiently impersonal. And that is precisely what it is not in neurotics, whose Oedipus complex has not passed through the correct process of transformation. Their super-ego still confronts their ego as a strict father confronts a child; and their morality operates in a primitive fashion in that the ego gets itself punished by the super-ego. Illness is employed as an instrument for this 'self-punishment', and neurotics have to behave as though they were governed by a sense of guilt which, in order to be satisfied, needs to be punished by illness.

'That really sounds most mysterious. The strangest thing about it is that apparently even this mighty force of the patient's conscience does not reach his consciousness.'

Yes, we are only beginning to appreciate the significance of all these important circumstances. That is why my description was bound to turn out so obscure. But now I can proceed. We describe all the forces that oppose the work of recovery as the patient's 'resistances'. The gain from illness is one such resistance. The 'unconscious sense of guilt' represents the super-ego's resistance; it is the most powerful factor, and the one most dreaded by us. We meet with still

---

[2][The charges of energy (cathexes) directed from the id on to its first external objects (the parents) are transformed into identifications and the objects are introduced into the ego and there take the form of a super-ego.]

other resistances during the treatment. If the ego during the early period has set up a repression out of fear, then the fear still persists and manifests itself as a resistance if the ego approaches the repressed material. And finally, as you can imagine, there are likely to be difficulties if an instinctual process which has been going along a particular path for whole decades is suddenly expected to take a new path that has just been made open for it. That might be called the id's resistance. The struggle against all these resistances is our main work during an analytic treatment; the task of making interpretations is nothing compared to it. But as a result of this struggle and of the overcoming of the resistances, the patient's ego is so much altered and strengthened that we can look forward calmly to his future behaviour when the treatment is over. On the other hand, you can understand now why we need such long treatments. The length of the path of development and the wealth of the material are not the decisive factors. It is more a question of whether the path is clear. An army can be held up for weeks on a stretch of country which in peace time an express crosses in a couple of hours—if the army has to overcome the enemy's resistance there. Such battles call for time in mental life too. I am unfortunately obliged to tell you that every effort to hasten analytic treatment appreciably has hitherto failed. The best way of shortening it seems to be to carry it out according to the rules.

'If I ever felt any desire to poach on your preserves and try my hand at analysing someone else, what you tell me about the resistances would have cured me of it. But how about the special personal influence that you yourself have after all admitted? Does not that come into action against the resistances?'

It is a good thing you have asked me about that. This personal influence is our most powerful dynamic weapon. It is the new element which we introduce into the situation and by means of which we make it fluid. The intellectual content of our explanations cannot do it, for the patient, who shares all the prejudices of the world around him, need believe us as little as our scientific critics do. The neurotic sets to work because he has faith in the analyst, and he believes him because he acquires a special emotional attitude towards the figure of the analyst. Children, too, only believe people they are attached to. I have already told you [pp. 9–10] what use we make of this particularly large 'suggestive' influence. Not for suppressing the symptoms—that distinguishes the analytic method from other psychotherapeutic procedures—but as a motive force to induce the patient to overcome his resistances.

'Well, and if that succeeds, does not everything then go smoothly?'

Yes, it ought to. But there turns out to be an unexpected complication. It was perhaps the greatest of the analyst's surprises to find that the emotional relation which the patient adopts towards him is of a quite peculiar nature. The very first doctor who attempted an analysis—it was not myself—came up against this phenomenon and did not know what to make of it. For this emotional relation is, to put it plainly, in the nature of falling in love. Strange, is it not? Especially when you take into account that the analyst does nothing to provoke it but on the contrary rather keeps at a distance from the patient, speaking humanly, and surrounds himself with some degree of reserve—when you learn besides that this odd love-relationship disregards anything else that is really propitious and every variation in personal attraction, age, sex, or class. This love is of a positively compulsive kind. Not that that characteristic need be absent from spontaneous falling in love. As you know, the contrary is often the case. But in the analytic situation it makes its appearance with complete regularity without there being any rational explanation for it. One would have thought that the patient's relation to the analyst called for no more than a certain amount of respect, trust, gratitude, and human sympathy. Instead, there is this falling in love, which itself gives the impression of being a pathological phenomenon.

'I should have thought all the same that it would be favourable for your analytic purposes. If someone is in love, he is amenable, and he will do anything in the world for the sake of the other person.'

Yes. It *is* favourable to start with. But when this falling in love has grown deeper, its whole nature comes to light, much of which is incompatible with the task of analysis. The patient's love is not satisfied with being obedient; it grows exacting, calls for affectionate and sensual satisfactions, it demands exclusiveness, it develops jealousy, and it shows more and more clearly its reverse side, its readiness to become hostile and revengeful if it cannot obtain its ends. At the same time, like all falling in love, it drives away all other mental material; it extinguishes interest in the treatment and in recovery—in short, there can be no doubt that it has taken the place of the neurosis and that our work has had the result of driving out one form of illness with another.

'That does sound hopeless! What can be done about it? The analysis would have to be given up. But if, as you say, the same thing happens in every case, it would be impossible to carry through any analyses at all.'

We will begin by using the situation in order to learn something from it. What we learn may then perhaps help us to master it. Is it not an extremely noteworthy fact that we succeed in transforming every neurosis, whatever its content, into a condition of pathological love?

Our conviction that a portion of erotic life that has been abnormally employed lies at the basis of neuroses must be unshakeably strengthened by this experience. With this discovery we are once more on a firm footing and can venture to make this love itself the object of analysis. And we can make another observation. Analytic love is not manifested in every case as clearly and blatantly as I have tried to depict it. Why not? We can soon see. In proportion as the purely sensual and the hostile sides of his love try to show themselves the patient's opposition to them is aroused. He struggles against them and tries to repress them before our very eyes. And now we understand what is happening. The patient is *repeating* in the form of falling in love with the analyst mental experiences which he has already been through once before; he has *transferred* on to the analyst mental attitudes that were lying ready in him and were intimately connected with his neurosis. He is also repeating before our eyes his old defensive actions; he would like best to repeat in his relation to the analyst *all* the history of that forgotten period of his life. So what he is showing us is the kernel of his intimate life history: *he is reproducing it tangibly, as though it were actually happening, instead of remembering it.* In this way the riddle of the transference-love is solved and the analysis can proceed on its way—with the *help* of the new situation which had seemed such a menace to it.

'That is very cunning. And is the patient so easy to convince that he is not in love but only obliged to stage a revival of an old piece?'

Everything now depends on that. And the whole skill in handling the 'transference' is devoted to bringing it about. As you see, the requirements of analytic technique reach their maximum at this point. Here the gravest mistakes can be made or the greatest successes be registered. It would be folly to attempt to evade the difficulties by suppressing or neglecting the transference: whatever else had been done in the treatment, it would not deserve the name of an analysis. To send the patient away as soon as the inconveniences of his transference-neurosis make their appearance would be no more sensible, and would moreover be cowardly. It would be as though one had conjured up spirits and run away from them as soon as they appeared. Sometimes, it is true, nothing else is possible. There are cases in which one cannot master the unleashed transference and the analysis has to be broken off; but one must at least have struggled with the evil spirits to the best of one's strength. To yield to the demands of the transference, to fulfil the patient's wishes for affectionate and sensual satisfaction, is not only justly forbidden by moral considerations but is also completely ineffective as a technical method for attaining the purpose of the analysis. A neurotic cannot be cured by being enabled to reproduce uncorrected an unconscious stereotype plate that is ready to hand in him. If one engages in compromises with him by offering him partial satisfactions in exchange for his further collaboration in the analysis, one must beware of falling into the ridiculous situation of the cleric who was supposed to convert a sick insurance agent. The sick man remained unconverted but the cleric took his leave insured. The only possible way out of the transference situation is to trace it back to the patient's past, as he really experienced it or as he pictured it through the wish-fulfilling activity of his imagination. And this demands from the analyst much skill, patience, calm, and self-abnegation.

'And where do you suppose the neurotic experienced the prototype of his transference-love?'

In his childhood: as a rule in his relation with one of his

parents. You will remember what importance we had to attribute to these earliest emotional ties. So here the circle closes.

'Have you finished at last? I am feeling just a little bewildered with all I have heard from you. Only tell me one thing more: how and where can one learn what is necessary for practising analysis?'

There are at the moment two Institutes at which instruction in psycho-analysis is given. The first has been founded in Berlin by Dr. Max Eitingon, who is a member of the Society there. The second is maintained by the Vienna Psycho-Analytical Society at its own expense and at considerable sacrifice. The part played by the authorities is at present limited to the many difficulties which they put in the way of the young undertaking. A third training Institute is at this moment being opened in London by the Society there, under the direction of Dr. Ernest Jones. At these Institutes the candidates themselves are taken into analysis, receive theoretical instruction by lectures on all the subjects that are important for them, and enjoy the supervision of older and more experienced analysts when they are allowed to make their first trials with comparatively slight cases. A period of some two years is calculated for this training. Even after this period, of course, the candidate is only a beginner and not yet a master. What is still needed must be acquired by practice and by an exchange of ideas in the psycho-analytical societies in which young and old members meet together. Preparation for analytic activity is by no means so easy and simple. The work is hard, the responsibility great. But anyone who has passed through such a course of instruction, who has been analysed himself, who has mastered what can be taught today of the psychology of the unconscious, who is at home in the science of sexual life, who has learnt the delicate technique of psycho-analysis, the art of interpretation, of fighting resistances, and of handling the transference—anyone who has accomplished all this *is no longer a layman in the field of psycho-analysis.* He is capable of undertaking the treatment of neurotic disorders, and will be able in time to achieve in that field whatever can be required from this form of therapy.

VI

'You have expended a great deal of effort on showing me
what psycho-analysis is and what sort of knowledge is needed
in order to practise it with some prospect of success. Very
well. Listening to you can have done me no harm. But I do
not know what influence on my judgement you expect your
explanations to have. I see before me a case which has
nothing unusual about it. The neuroses are a particular kind
of illness and analysis is a particular method of treating
them—a specialized branch of medicine. It is the rule in
other cases as well for a doctor who has chosen a special
branch of medicine not to be satisfied with the education
that is confirmed by his diploma: particularly if he intends
to set up in a fairly large town, such as can alone offer a
livelihood to specialists. Anyone who wants to be a surgeon
tries to work for a few years at a surgical clinic, and similarly
with oculists, laryngologists, and so on—to say nothing of
psychiatrists, who are perhaps never able to get away from
a state institution or a sanatorium. And the same will happen in the case of psycho-analysts: anyone who decides in
favour of this new specialized branch of medicine will, when
his studies are completed, take on the two years' training you
spoke of in a training institute, if it really requires so much
time. He will realize afterwards, too, that it is to his advantage to keep up his contact with his colleagues in a psycho-

analytical society, and everything will go along swimmingly. I cannot see where there is a place in this for the question of lay analysis.'

A doctor who does what you have promised on his behalf will be welcome to all of us. Four-fifths of those whom I recognize as my pupils are in any case doctors. But allow me to point out to you how the relations of doctors to analysis have really developed and how they will probably continue to develop. Doctors have no historical claim to the sole possession of analysis. On the contrary, until recently they have met it with everything possible that could damage it, from the shallowest ridicule to the gravest calumny. You will justly reply that that belongs to the past and need not affect the future. I agree, but I fear the future will be different from what you have foretold.

Permit me to give the word 'quack' the meaning it ought to have instead of the legal one. According to the law a quack is anyone who treats patients without possessing a state diploma to prove he is a doctor. I should prefer another definition: a quack is anyone who undertakes a treatment without possessing the knowledge and capacities necessary for it. Taking my stand on this definition, I venture to assert that—not only in European countries—doctors form a preponderating contingent of quacks in analysis. They very frequently practise analytic treatment without having learnt it and without understanding it.

It is no use your objecting that that is unconscientious and that you cannot believe doctors capable of it; that after all a doctor knows that a medical diploma is not a letter of marque[1] and that a patient is not an outlaw; and that one must always grant to a doctor that he is acting in good faith even if he may perhaps be in error.

The facts remain; we will hope that they can be ac-

---

[1] [i.e., does not give him a privateer's licence.]

counted for as you think. I will try to explain to you how it becomes possible for a doctor to act in connexion with psycho-analysis in a manner which he would carefully avoid in every other field.

The first consideration is that in his medical school a doctor receives a training which is more or less the opposite of what he would need as a preparation for psycho-analysis. His attention has been directed to objectively ascertainable facts of anatomy, physics, and chemistry, on the correct appreciation and suitable influencing of which the success of medical treatment depends. The problem of life is brought into his field of vision so far as it has hitherto been explained to us by the play of forces which can also be observed in inanimate nature. His interest is not aroused in the mental side of vital phenomena; medicine is not concerned with the study of the higher intellectual functions, which lies in the sphere of another faculty. Only psychiatry is supposed to deal with the disturbances of mental functions; but we know in what manner and with what aims it does so. It looks for the somatic determinants of mental disorders and treats them like other causes of illness.

Psychiatry is right to do so and medical education is clearly excellent. If it is described as one-sided, one must first discover the standpoint from which one is making that characteristic into a reproach. In itself every science is one-sided. It must be so, since it restricts itself to particular subjects, points of view, and methods. It is a piece of nonsense in which I would take no part to play off one science against another. After all, physics does not diminish the value of chemistry; it cannot take its place but on the other hand cannot be replaced by it. Psycho-analysis is certainly quite particularly one-sided, as being the science of the mental unconscious. We must not therefore dispute to the medical sciences their right to be one-sided.

We shall only find the standpoint we are in search of if we turn from scientific medicine to practical therapeutics. A sick person is a complicated organism. He may remind us that even the mental phenomena which are so hard to grasp should not be effaced from the picture of life. Neurotics, indeed, are an undesired complication, an embarrassment as much to therapeutics as to jurisprudence and to military service. But they exist and are a particular concern of medicine. Medical education, however, does nothing, literally nothing, towards their understanding and treatment. In view of the intimate connexion between the things that we distinguish as physical and mental, we may look forward to a day when paths of knowledge and, let us hope, of influence will be opened up, leading from organic biology and chemistry to the field of neurotic phenomena. That day still seems a distant one, and for the present these illnesses are inaccessible to us from the direction of medicine.

It would be tolerable if medical education merely failed to give doctors any orientation in the field of the neuroses. But it does more: it gives them a false and detrimental attitude. Doctors whose interest has not been aroused in the psychical factors of life are all too ready to form a low estimate of them and to ridicule them as unscientific. For that reason they are unable to take anything really seriously which has to do with them and do not recognize the obligations which derive from them. They therefore fall into the layman's lack of respect for psychological research and make their own task easy for themselves.—No doubt neurotics have to be treated, since they are sick people and come to the doctor; and one must always be ready to experiment with something new. But why burden oneself with a tedious preparation? We shall manage all right; who can tell if what they teach in the analytic institutes is any good?—The less such doctors understand about the matter, the more venturesome they become. Only a man who really knows is modest, for he knows how insufficient his knowledge is.

The comparison which you brought up to pacify me, between specialization in analysis and in other branches of medicine, is thus not applicable. For surgery, ophthalmology, and so on, the medical school itself offers an opportunity for further education. The analytic training institutes are few in number, young in years, and without authority. The medical schools have not recognized them and take no notice of them. The young doctor, who has had to take so much on trust from his teachers that he has had little occasion for educating his judgement, will gladly seize an occasion for playing the part of a critic for once in a field in which there is as yet no recognized authority.

There are other things too that favour his appearing as an analytic quack. If he tried to undertake eye-operations without sufficient preparation, the failure of his cataract extractions and iridectomies and the absence of patients would soon bring his hazardous enterprise to an end. The practice of analysis is comparatively safe for him. The public is spoilt by the average successful outcome of eye-operations and expects cure from the surgeon. But if a 'nerve-specialist' fails to restore his patients no one is surprised. People have not been spoilt by successes in the therapy of the neuroses; the nerve-specialist has at least 'taken a lot of trouble with them'. Indeed, there is not much that can be done; nature must help, or time. With women there is first menstruation, then marriage, and later on the menopause. Finally death is a real help. Moreover, what the medical analyst has done with his neurotic patient is so inconspicuous that no reproach can attach to it. He has made use of no instruments or medicines; he has merely conversed with him and tried to talk him into or out of something. Surely that can do no harm, especially if he avoids touching on distressing or agitating subjects. The medical analyst, who has avoided any strict teaching, will, no doubt, not have omitted an attempt to improve analysis, to pull out its poison fangs and make it pleasant for the patient. And it will be wise for him to stop there: for if he really ventures to call up resistances and then does not know how to meet them, he may in true earnest make himself unpopular.

Honesty compels me to admit that the activity of an untrained analyst does less harm to his patients than that of an unskilled surgeon. The possible damage is limited to the patient having been led into useless expenditure and having his chances of recovery removed or diminished. Furthermore, the reputation of analytic therapy has been lowered. All this is most undesirable, but it bears no comparison with the dangers that threaten from the knife of a surgical quack. In my judgement, severe or permanent aggravations of a pathological condition are not to be feared even with an unskilled use of analysis. The unwelcome reactions cease after a while. Compared with the traumas of life which have provoked the illness, a little mishandling by the doctor is of no account. It is simply that the unsuitable attempt at a cure has done the patient no good.

'I have listened to your account of the medical quack in analysis without interrupting you, though I formed an impression that you are dominated by a hostility against the medical profession to the historical explanation of which you yourself have pointed the way. But I will grant you one thing: if analyses are to be carried out, it should be by people who have been thoroughly trained for it. And do you not think that with time the doctors who turn to analysis will do everything to obtain that training?'

I fear not. So long as the attitude of the medical school

to the analytic training institute remains unaltered, doctors will find the temptation to make things easier for themselves too great.

'But you seem to be consistently evading any direct pronouncement on the question of lay analysis. What I guess now is that, because it is impossible to keep a check on doctors who want to analyse, you are proposing, out of revenge, as it were, to punish them by depriving them of their monopoly in analysis and by throwing open this medical activity to laymen as well.'

I cannot say whether you have guessed my motives correctly. Perhaps I shall be able later on to put evidence before you of a less partial attitude. But I lay stress on the demand that *no one should practise analysis who has not acquired the right to do so by a particular training*. Whether such a person is a doctor or not seems to me immaterial.

'Then what definite proposals have you to make?'

I have not got so far as that yet; and I cannot tell whether I shall get there at all. I should like to discuss another question with you, and first of all to touch on one special point. It is said that the authorities, at the instigation of the medical profession, want to forbid the practice of analysis by laymen altogether. Such a prohibition would also affect the non-medical members of the Psycho-Analytical Society, who have enjoyed an excellent training and have perfected themselves greatly by practice. If the prohibition were enacted, we should find ourselves in a position in which a number of people are prevented from carrying out an activity which one can safely feel convinced they can perform very well, while the same activity is opened to other people for whom there is no question of a similar guarantee. That is not precisely the sort of result to which legislation should lead. However, this special problem is neither very important nor difficult to solve. Only a handful of people are concerned, who cannot be seriously damaged. They will probably emigrate to Germany where no legislation will prevent them from finding recognition for their proficiency. If it is desired to spare them this and to mitigate the law's severity, that can easily be done on the basis of some well-known precedents. Under the Austrian Monarchy it repeatedly happened that permission was given to notorious quacks, *ad personam* [personally], to carry out medical activities in certain fields, because people were convinced of their real ability. Those concerned were for the most part peasant healers, and their recommendation seems regularly to have been made by one of the Archduchesses who were once so numerous; but it ought to be possible for it also to be done in the case of town-dwellers and on the basis of a different and merely expert guarantee. Such a prohibition would have more important effects on the Vienna analytic training institute, which would thenceforward be unable to accept any candidates for training from non-medical circles. Thus once again in our country a line of intellectual activity would be suppressed which is allowed to develop freely elsewhere. I am the last person to claim any competence in judging laws and regulations. But this much I can see: that to lay emphasis on our quackery law does not lead in the direction of the approach to conditions in Germany which is so much aimed at today,[2] and that the application of that law to the case of psycho-analysis has something of an anachronism about it, since at the time of its enactment there was as yet no such thing as analysis and the peculiar nature of neurotic illnesses was not yet recognized.

I come now to a question the discussion of which seems to me more important. Is the practice of psycho-analysis a matter which should in general be subject to official interfer-

---

[2][This of course was in the days of the Weimar republic.]

ence, or would it be more expedient to leave it to follow its natural development? I shall certainly not come to any decision on this point here and now, but I shall take the liberty of putting the problem before you for your consideration. In our country from of old a positive *furor prohibendi* [passion for prohibitions] has been the rule, a tendency to keep people under tutelage, to interfere and to forbid, which, as we all know, has not borne particularly good fruit. In our new republican Austria, it seems things have not yet changed very much. I fancy you will have an important word to say in deciding the case of psycho-analysis which we are now considering; I do not know whether you have the wish or the influence with which to oppose these bureaucratic tendencies. At all events, I shall not spare you my unauthoritative thoughts on the subject. In my opinion a superabundance of regulations and prohibitions injures the authority of the law. It can be observed that where only a few prohibitions exist they are carefully observed, but where one is accompanied by prohibitions at every step, one feels definitely tempted to disregard them. Moreover, it does not mean one is quite an anarchist if one is prepared to realize that laws and regulations cannot from their origin claim to possess the attribute of being sacred and untransgressable, that they are often inadequately framed and offend our sense of justice, or will do so after a time, and that, in view of the sluggishness of the authorities, there is often no other means of correcting such inexpedient laws than by boldly violating them. Furthermore, if one desires to maintain respect for laws and regulations it is advisable not to enact any where a watch cannot easily be kept on whether they are obeyed or transgressed. Much of what I have quoted above on the practice of analysis by doctors could be repeated here in regard to genuine analysis by laymen which the law is seeking to suppress. The course of analysis is most inconspicuous, it employs neither medicines nor instruments and consists only in talking and an exchange of information; it will not be easy to prove that a layman is practising 'analysis' if he asserts that he is merely giving encouragement and explanations and trying to establish a healthy human influence on people who are in search of mental assistance. It would surely not be possible to forbid that merely because doctors sometimes do the same thing. In English-speaking countries the practices of Christian Science have become very widespread: a kind of dialectical denial of the evils in life, based on an appeal to the doctrines of the Christian religion. I do not hesitate to assert that that procedure represents a regrettable aberration of the human spirit; but who in America or England would dream of forbidding it and making it punishable? Are the authorities so certain of the right path to salvation that they venture to prevent each man from trying 'to be saved after his own fashion'?[3] And granted that many people if they are left to themselves run into danger and come to grief, would not the authorities do better carefully to mark the limits of the regions which are to be regarded as not to be trespassed upon, and for the rest, so far as possible, to allow human beings to be educated by experience and mutual influence? Psycho-analysis is something so new in the world, the mass of mankind is so little instructed about it, the attitude of official science to it is still so vacillating, that it seems to me over-hasty to intervene in its development with legislative regulations. Let us allow patients themselves to discover that it is damaging to them to look for mental assistance to people who have not learnt how to give it. If we explain this to them and warn them against it, we shall have spared ourselves the need to forbid

---

[3] [The saying 'In my State every man can be saved after his own fashion' is attributed to Frederick the Great.]

it. On the main roads of Italy the pylons that carry high-
tension cables bear the brief and impressive inscription: 'Chi
tocca, muore [He who touches will die].' This is perfectly
calculated to regulate the behaviour of passers-by to any
wires that may be hanging down. The corresponding German notices exhibit an unnecessary and offensive verbosity:
'Das Berühren der Leitungsdrähte ist, weil lebensgefährlich,
strengstens verboten [Touching the transmission cables is,
since it is dangerous to life, most strictly prohibited].' Why
the prohibition? Anyone who holds his life dear will make
the prohibition for himself; and anyone who wants to kill
himself in that way will not ask for permission.

'But there are instances that can be quoted as legal precedents against allowing lay analysis; I mean the prohibition
against laymen practising hypnotism and the recently
enacted prohibition against holding spiritualist séances or
founding spiritualist societies.'

I cannot say that I am an admirer of these measures. The
second one is a quite undisguised encroachment of police
supervision to the detriment of intellectual freedom. I am
beyond suspicion of having much belief in what are known
as 'occult phenomena' or of feeling any desire that they
should be recognized. But prohibitions like these will not
stifle people's interest in that supposedly mysterious world.
They may on the contrary have done much harm and have
closed the door to an impartial curiosity which might have
arrived at a judgement that would have set us free from
these harassing possibilities. But once again this only applies
to Austria. In other countries 'para-psychical' researches are
not met by any legal obstacles. The case of hypnotism is
somewhat different from that of analysis. Hypnotism is the
evoking of an abnormal mental state and is used by laymen
today only for the purpose of public shows. If hypnotic
therapy had maintained its very promising beginnings a

position would have been arrived at similar to that of analysis. And incidentally the history of hypnotism provides a precedent for that of analysis in another direction. When I was a young lecturer in neuropathology, the doctors inveighed passionately against hypnotism, declared that it was a swindle, a deception of the Devil's, and a highly dangerous procedure. Today they have monopolized this same hypnotism and they make use of it unhesitatingly as a method of examination; for some nerve specialists it is still their chief therapeutic instrument.

But I have already told you that I have no intention of making proposals which are based on the decision as to whether legal control or letting things go is to be preferred in the matter of analysis. I know this is a question of principle on the reply to which the inclinations of persons in authority will probably have more influence than arguments. I have already set out what seems to me to speak in favour of a policy of *laissez faire.* If the other decision is taken—for a policy of active intervention—then it seems to me that in any case a lame and unjust measure of ruthlessly forbidding analysis by non-doctors will be an insufficient outcome. More will have to be considered in that case: the conditions will have to be laid down under which the practice of analysis shall be permitted to all those who seek to make use of it, an authority will have to be set up from whom one can learn what analysis is and what sort of preparation is needed for it, and the possibilities for instruction in analysis will have to be encouraged. We must therefore either leave things alone or establish order and clarity; we must not rush into a complicated situation with a single isolated prohibition derived mechanically from a regulation that has become inadequate.

VII

'Yes, but the doctors! the doctors! I cannot induce you to go into the real subject of our conversations. You still keep on evading me. It is a question of whether we should not give doctors the exclusive right of practising analysis—for all I care, after they have fulfilled certain conditions. The majority of doctors are certainly not quacks in analysis as you have represented them. You say yourself that the great majority of your pupils and followers are doctors. It has come to my ears that they are far from sharing your point of view on the question of lay analysis. I may no doubt assume that your pupils agree with your demands for sufficient preparation and so on; and yet these pupils think it consistent to close the practice of analysis to laymen. Is that so? and if so, how do you explain it?'

I see you are well informed. Yes, it is so. Not all, it is true, but a good proportion of my medical colleagues do not agree with me over this, and are in favour of doctors having an exclusive right to the analytic treatment of neurotics. This will show you that differences of opinion are allowed even in our camp. The side I take is well-known, and the contradiction on the subject of lay analysis does not interfere with our good understanding. How can I explain the attitude of these pupils of mine to you? I do not know for certain; I think it must be the power of professional feeling. The course of their development has been different from mine, they still feel uncomfortable in their isolation from their colleagues, they would like to be accepted by the 'profession' as having plenary rights, and are prepared, in exchange for that tolerance, to make a sacrifice at a point whose vital importance is not obvious to them. Perhaps it may be otherwise; to impute motives of competition to them would be not only to accuse them of base sentiments but also to attribute a strange shortsightedness to them. They are always ready to introduce other doctors into analysis, and from a material point of view it must be a matter of indifference to them whether they have to share the available patients with medical colleagues or with laymen. But something different probably plays a part. These pupils of mine may be influenced by certain factors which guarantee a doctor an undoubted advantage over a layman in analytic practice.

'Guarantee him an advantage? There we have it. So you are admitting the advantage at last? This should settle the question.'

The admission is not hard for me to make. It may show you that I am not so passionately prejudiced as you suppose. I have put off mentioning these things because their discussion will once again make theoretical considerations necessary.

'What are you thinking of now?'

First there is the question of diagnosis. When one takes into analysis a patient suffering from what are described as nervous disorders, one wishes beforehand to be certain—so far, of course, as certainty can be attained—that he is suited for this kind of treatment, that one can help him, that is to say, by this method. That, however, is only the case if he really has a neurosis.

'I should have thought that would be recognizable from

the phenomena, the symptoms, of which he complains.'

This is where a fresh complication arises. It cannot always be recognized with complete certainty. The patient may exhibit the external picture of a neurosis, and yet it may be something else—the beginning of an incurable mental disease or the preliminary of a destructive process in the brain. The distinction—the differential diagnosis—is not always easy and cannot be made immediately in every phase. The responsibility for such a decision can of course only be undertaken by a doctor. As I have said, it is not always easy for him. The illness may have an innocent appearance for a considerable time, till in the end it after all displays its evil character. Indeed, it is one of the regular fears of neurotics that they may become insane. However, if a doctor has been mistaken for a time over a case of this sort or has been in uncertainty about it, no harm has been caused and nothing unnecessary has been done. Nor indeed would the analytic treatment of this case have done any harm, though it would have been exposed as an unnecessary waste. And moreover there would certainly be enough people who would blame the analysis for the unfortunate outcome. Unjustly, no doubt, but such occasions ought to be avoided.

'But that sounds hopeless. It strikes at the roots of everything you have told me about the nature and origin of a neurosis.'

Not at all. It merely confirms once again the fact that neurotics are a nuisance and an embarrassment for all concerned—including the analysts. But perhaps I shall clear up your confusion if I state my new information in more correct terms. It would probably be more correct to say of the cases we are now dealing with that they have really developed a neurosis, but that it is not psychogenic but somatogenic—that its causes are not mental but physical. Do you understand?

'Oh, yes, I understand. But I cannot bring it into harmony with the other side, the psychological one.'

That can be managed, though, if one bears in mind the complexities of living substance. In what did we find the essence of a neurosis? In the fact that the ego, the higher organization of the mental apparatus (elevated through the influence of the external world), is not able to fulfil its function of mediating between the id and reality, that in its feebleness it draws back from some instinctual portions of the id and, to make up for this, has to put up with the consequences of its renunciation in the form of restrictions, symptoms, and unsuccessful reaction-formations.

A feebleness of the ego of this sort is to be found in all of us in childhood; and that is why the experiences of the earliest years of childhood are of such great importance for later life. Under the extraordinary burden of this period of childhood—we have in a few years to cover the enormous developmental distance between stone-age primitive men and the participants in contemporary civilization, and, at the same time and in particular, we have to fend off the instinctual impulses of the early sexual period—under this burden, then, our ego takes refuge in repression and lays itself open to a childhood neurosis, the precipitate of which it carries with it into maturity as a disposition to a later nervous illness. Everything now depends on how the growing organism is treated by fate. If life becomes too hard, if the gulf between instinctual claims and the demands of reality becomes too great, the ego may fail in its efforts to reconcile the two, and the more readily, the more it is inhibited by the disposition carried over by it from infancy. The process of repression is then repeated, the instincts tear themselves away from the ego's domination, find their substitutive satisfactions along the paths of regression, and the poor ego has become helplessly neurotic.

Only let us hold fast to this: the nodal point and pivot of the whole situation is the relative strength of the ego organization. We shall then find it easy to complete our aetiological survey. As what may be called the normal causes of neurotic illness we already know the feebleness of the childhood ego, the task of dealing with the early sexual impulses, and the effects of the more or less chance experiences of childhood. Is it not possible, however, that yet other factors play a part, derived from the time before the beginning of the child's life? For instance, an innate strength and unruliness of the instinctual life in the id, which from the outset sets the ego tasks too hard for it? Or a special developmental feebleness of the ego due to unknown reasons? Such factors must of course acquire an aetiological importance, in some cases a transcendent one. We have invariably to reckon with the instinctual strength of the id; if it has developed to excess, the prospects of our therapy are poor. We still know too little of the causes of a developmental inhibition of the ego. These then would be the cases of neurosis with an essentially constitutional basis. Without some such constitutional, congenital favouring factors a neurosis can, no doubt, scarcely come about.

But if the relative feebleness of the ego is the decisive factor for the genesis of a neurosis, it must also be possible for a later physical illness to produce a neurosis, provided that it can bring about an enfeeblement of the ego. And that, once again, is very frequently found. A physical disorder of this kind can affect the instinctual life in the id and increase the strength of the instincts beyond the limit up to which the ego is capable of coping with them. The normal model of such processes is perhaps the alteration in women caused by the disturbances of menstruation and the menopause. Or again, a general somatic illness, indeed an organic disease of the nervous central organ, may attack the nutritional conditions of the mental apparatus and compel it to reduce its functioning and to bring to a halt its more delicate workings, one of which is the maintenance of the ego organization. In all these cases approximately the same picture of neurosis emerges; neurosis always has the same psychological mechanism, but, as we see, a most varied and often very complex aetiology.

'You please me better now. You have begun talking like a doctor at last. And now I expect you to admit that such a complicated medical affair as a neurosis can only be handled by a doctor.'

I fear you are overshooting the mark. What we have been discussing was a piece of pathology, what we are concerned with in analysis is a therapeutic procedure. I allow—no, I insist—that in every case which is under consideration for analysis the diagnosis shall be established first by a doctor. By far the greater number of neuroses which occupy us are fortunately of a psychogenic nature and give no grounds for pathological suspicions. Once the doctor has established this, he can confidently hand over the treatment to a lay analyst. In our analytical societies matters have always been arranged in that way. Thanks to the intimate contact between medical and non-medical members, mistakes such as might be feared have been as good as completely avoided. There is a further contingency, again, in which the analyst has to ask the doctor's help. In the course of an analytic treatment, symptoms—most often physical symptoms— may appear about which one is doubtful whether they should be regarded as belonging to the neurosis or whether they should be related to an independent organic illness that has intervened. The decision on this point must once again be left to a doctor.

'So that even during the course of analysis a lay analyst cannot do without a doctor. A fresh argument against their fitness.'

No. No argument against lay analysts can be manufactured out of this possibility, for in such circumstances a medical analyst would not act differently.

'I do not understand that.'

There is a technical rule that an analyst, if dubious symptoms like this emerge during the treatment, shall not submit them to his own judgement but shall get them reported upon by a doctor who is not connected with analysis—a consultant physician, perhaps—even if the analyst himself is a doctor and still well-versed in his medical knowledge.

'And why should a rule be made that seems to me so uncalled-for?'

It is not uncalled-for; in fact there are several reasons for it. In the first place it is not a good plan for a combination of organic and psychical treatment to be carried out by one and the same person. Secondly the relation in the transference may make it inadvisable for the analyst to examine the patient physically. And thirdly the analyst has every reason for doubting whether he is unprejudiced, since his interests are directed so intensely to the psychical factors.

'I now understand your attitude to lay analysis quite clearly. You are determined that there must be lay analysts. And since you cannot dispute their inadequacy for their task, you are scraping together everything you can to excuse them and make their existence easier. But I cannot in the least see why there should be lay analysts, who, after all, can only be therapists of the second class. I am ready, so far as I am concerned, to make an exception in the case of the few laymen who have already been trained as analysts; but no fresh ones should be created and the training institutes should be put under an obligation to take no more laymen into training.'

I am at one with you, if it can be shown that all the interests involved will be served by this restriction. You will agree that these interests are of three sorts: that of the patients, that of the doctors, and—last but not least—that of science, which indeed comprises the interests of all future patients. Shall we examine these three points together?

For the patient, then, it is a matter of indifference whether the analyst is a doctor or not, provided only that the danger of his condition being misunderstood is excluded by the necessary medical reports before the treatment begins and on some possible occasions during the course of it. For him it is incomparably more important that the analyst should possess personal qualities that make him trustworthy, and that he should have acquired the knowledge and understanding as well as the experience which alone can make it possible for him to fulfill his task. It might be thought that it would damage an analyst's authority if the patient knows that he is not a doctor and cannot in some situations do without a doctor's support. We have, of course, never omitted to inform patients of their analyst's qualification, and we have been able to convince ourselves that professional prejudices find no echo in them and that they are ready to accept a cure from whatever direction it is offered them—which, incidentally, the medical profession discovered long ago to its deep mortification. Nor are the lay analysts who practise analysis today any chance collection of riffraff, but people of academic education, doctors of philosophy, educationists, together with a few women of great experience in life and outstanding personality. The analysis, to which all the candidates in an analytic training institute have to submit, is at the same time the best means of forming an opinion of their personal aptitude for carrying out their exacting occupation.

Now as to the interest of the doctors. I cannot think that it would gain by the incorporation of psycho-analysis into medicine. The medical curriculum already lasts for five years and the final examinations extend well into a sixth year. Every few years fresh demands are made on the student, without the fulfillment of which his equipment for the future would have to be declared insufficient. Access to the medical profession is very difficult and its practice neither satisfying nor very remunerative. If one supports what is certainly a fully justified demand that doctors should also be familiar with the mental side of illness, and if on that account one extends medical education to include some preparation for analysis, that implies a further increase in the curriculum and a corresponding prolongation of the period of study. I do not know whether the doctors will be pleased by this consequence of their claim upon analysis. But it can scarcely be escaped. And this at a period in which the conditions of material existence have so greatly deteriorated for the classes from which doctors are recruited, a period in which the younger generation sees itself compelled to make itself self-supporting as early in life as possible.

But perhaps you will choose not to burden medical studies with the preparation for analytic practice but think it more expedient for future analysts to take up their necessary training only after the end of their medical studies. You may say the loss of time involved in this is of no practical account, since after all a young man of less than thirty will never enjoy his patients' confidence, which is a *sine qua non* of giving mental assistance. It might no doubt be said in reply that a newly-fledged physician for physical illnesses cannot count upon being treated by his patients with very great respect either, and that a young analyst might very well fill in his time by working in a psycho-analytic out-patient clinic under the supervision of experienced practitioners.

But what seems to me more important is that with this proposal of yours you are giving support to a waste of energy for which, in these difficult times, I can really find no economic justification. Analytic training, it is true, cuts across the field of medical education, but neither includes the other. If—which may sound fantastic today—one had to found a college of psycho-analysis, much would have to be taught in it which is also taught by the medical faculty. alongside of depth-psychology, which would always remain the principal subject, there would be an introduction to biology, as much as possible of the science of sexual life, and familiarity with the symptomatology of psychiatry. On the other hand, analytic instruction would include branches of knowledge which are remote from medicine and which the doctor does not come across in his practice: the history of civilization, mythology, the psychology of religion and the science of literature. Unless he is well at home in these subjects, an analyst can make nothing of a large amount of his material. By way of compensation, the great mass of what is taught in medical schools is of no use to him for his purposes. A knowledge of the anatomy of the tarsal bones, of the constitution of the carbohydrates, of the course of the cranial nerves, a grasp of all that medicine has brought to light on bacilli as exciting causes of disease and the means of combating them, on serum reactions and on neoplasms— all this knowledge, which is undoubtedly of the highest value in itself, is nevertheless of no consequence to him; it does not concern him; it neither helps him directly to understand a neurosis and to cure it nor does it contribute to a sharpening of those intellectual capacities on which his occupation makes the greatest demands. It cannot be objected that the case is much the same when a doctor takes up some other special branch of medicine—dentistry, for instance: in that case, too, he may not need some of what he has to pass examinations in, and he will have to learn much in addition, for which his schooling has not prepared him. But the two cases cannot be put on a par. In dentistry the great principles of pathology—the theories of inflammation, suppuration, necrosis, and of the metabolism of the bodily organs—still retain their importance. But the experience of an analyst lies in another world, with other phenomena and other laws. However much philosophy may ignore the gulf between the physical and the mental, it still exists for our immediate experience and still more for our practical endeavours.

It is unjust and inexpedient to try to compel a person who wants to set someone else free from the torment of a phobia or an obsession to take the roundabout road of the medical curriculum. Nor will such an endeavour have any success, unless it results in suppressing analysis entirely. Imagine a landscape in which two paths lead to a hilltop with a view—one short and straight, the other long, winding, and circuitous. You try to stop up the short path by a prohibitory notice, perhaps because it passes by some flower-beds that you want to protect. The only chance you have of your prohibition being respected is if the short path is steep and difficult while the longer one leads gently up. If, however, that is not so, and the roundabout path is on the contrary the harder, you may imagine the value of your prohibition and the fate of your flower-beds! I fear you will succeed in compelling the laymen to study medicine just as little as I shall be able to induce doctors to learn analysis. For you know human nature as well as I do.

'If you are right, that analytic treatment cannot be carried out without special training, but that the medical curriculum cannot bear the further burden of a preparation for it, and that medical knowledge is to a great extent unnecessary for an analyst, how shall we achieve the ideal physician who shall be equal to all the tasks of his calling?'

I cannot foresee the way out of these difficulties, nor is it my business to point it out. I see only two things: first that analysis is an embarrassment to you and that the best thing would be for it not to exist—though neurotics, no doubt, are an embarrassment too; and secondly, that the interests of everyone concerned would for the time being be met if the doctors could make up their minds to tolerate a class of therapists which would relieve them of the tedium of treating the enormously common psychogenic neuroses while remaining in constant touch with them to the benefit of the patients.

'Is that your last word on the subject? or have you something more to say?'

Yes indeed. I wanted to bring up a third interest—the interest of science. What I have to say about that will concern you little; but, by comparison, it is of all the more importance to me.

For we do not consider it at all desirable for psychoanalysis to be swallowed up by medicine and to find its last resting-place in a text-book of psychiatry under the heading 'Methods of Treatment', alongside of procedures such as hypnotic suggestion, autosuggestion, and persuasion, which, born from our ignorance, have to thank the laziness and cowardice of mankind for their short-lived effects. It deserves a better fate and it may be hoped, will meet with one. As a 'depth-psychology', a theory of the mental unconscious, it can become indispensable to all the sciences which are concerned with the evolution of human civilization and its major institutions such as art, religion, and the social order. It has already, in my opinion, afforded these sciences considerable help in solving their problems. But these are only small contributions compared with what might be achieved if historians of civilization, psychologists of religion, philologists, and so on would agree themselves to handle the new instrument of research which is at their service. The use of analysis for the treatment of the neuroses is only one of its applications; the future will perhaps show that it is not the most important one. In any case it would be wrong to sacrifice all the other applications to this single one, just because it touches on the circle of medical interests.

For here a further prospect stretches ahead, which cannot be encroached upon with impunity. If the representatives of the various mental sciences are to study psycho-analysis so as to be able to apply its methods and angles of approach to their own material, it will not be enough for them to stop short at the findings which are laid down in analytic literature. They must learn to understand analysis in the only way that is possible—by themselves undergoing an analysis. The neurotics who need analysis would thus be joined by a second class of persons, who accept analysis from intellectual motives, but who will no doubt also welcome the increase in their capacities which they will incidentally achieve. To carry out these analyses a number of analysts will be needed, for whom any medical knowledge will have particularly little importance. But these 'teaching analysts'—let us call them—will require to have had a particularly careful education. If this is not to be stunted, they must be given an opportunity of collecting experience from instructive and informative cases; and since healthy people who also lack the motive of curiosity do not present themselves for analysis, it is once more only upon neurotics that it will be possible for the teaching analysts—under careful supervision—to be educated for their subsequent non-medical activity. All this, however, requires a certain amount of freedom of movement, and is not compatible with petty restrictions.

Perhaps you do not believe in these purely theoretical

interests of psycho-analysis or cannot allow them to affect the practical question of lay analysis. Then let me advise you that psycho-analysis has yet another sphere of application, which is outside the scope of the quackery law and to which the doctors will scarcely lay claim. Its application, I mean, to the bringing-up of children. If a child begins to show signs of an undesirable development, if it grows moody, refractory, and inattentive, the paediatrician and even the school doctor can do nothing for it, even if the child produces clear neurotic symptoms, such as nervousness, loss of appetite, vomiting, or insomnia. A treatment that combines analytic influence with educational measures, carried out by people who are not ashamed to concern themselves with the affairs in a child's world, and who understand how to find their way into a child's mental life, can bring about two things at once: the removal of the neurotic symptoms and the reversal of the change in character which had begun. Our recognition of the importance of these inconspicuous neuroses of children as laying down the disposition for serious illnesses in later life points to these child analyses as an excellent method of prophylaxis. Analysis undeniably still has its enemies. I do not know whether they have means at their command for stopping the activities of these educational analysts or analytic educationalists. I do not think it very likely; but one can never feel too secure.

Moreover, to return to our question of the analytic treatment of adult neurotics, even there we have not yet exhausted every line of approach. Our civilization imposes an almost intolerable pressure on us and it calls for a corrective. Is it too fantastic to expect that psycho-analysis in spite of its difficulties may be destined to the task of preparing mankind for such a corrective? Perhaps once more an American may hit on the idea of spending a little money to get the 'social workers' of his country trained analytically and to turn them into a band of helpers for combating the neuroses of civilization.

'Aha! a new kind of Salvation Army!'

Why not? Our imagination always follows patterns. The stream of eager learners who will then flow to Europe will be obliged to pass Vienna by, for here the development of analysis may have succumbed to a premature trauma of prohibition. You smile? I am not saying this as a bribe for your support. Not in the least. I know you do not believe me; nor can I guarantee that it will happen. But one thing I do know. It is by no means so important *what* decision you give on the question of lay analysis. It may have a local effect. But the things that really matter—the possibilities in psycho-analysis for *internal* development—can never be affected by regulations and prohibitions

POSTSCRIPT (1927)

_____

The immediate occasion of my writing the small volume which was the starting-point of the present discussion was a charge of quackery brought against a non-medical member of our Society, Dr. Theodor Reik, in the Vienna Courts. It is generally known, I think, that after all the preliminary proceedings had been completed and a number of expert opinions had been received, the charge was dropped. I do not believe that this was a result of my book. No doubt the prosecution's case was too weak, and the person who brought the charge as an aggrieved party proved an untrustworthy witness. So that the quashing of the proceedings against Dr. Reik is probably not to be regarded as a considered judgement of the Vienna Courts on the general question of lay analysis. When I drew the figure of the 'Impartial Person' who was my interlocutor in my tract, I had before my mind one of our high officials. This was a man with a friendly attitude and a mind of unusual integrity, to whom I had myself talked about Reik's case and for whom I had, at his request, written a confidential opinion on the subject. I knew I had not succeeded in converting him to my views, and that was why I made my dialogue with the Impartial Person end without agreement too.

Nor did I expect that I should succeed in bringing about

unanimity in the attitude of analysts themselves towards the problem of lay analysis. Anyone who compares the views expressed by the Hungarian Society in this discussion with those of the New York group will perhaps conclude that my book has produced no effect whatever and that everyone persists in his former opinion. But I do not believe this either. I think that many of my colleagues have modified their extreme *parti pris* and that the majority have accepted my view that the problem of lay analysis ought not to be decided along the lines of traditional usage but that it arises from a novel situation and therefore demands a fresh judgement.

Again, the turn which I gave to the whole discussion seems to have met with approval. My main thesis was that the important question is not whether an analyst possesses a medical diploma but whether he has had the special training necessary for the practice of analysis. This served as the starting-point for a discussion, which was eagerly embarked upon, as to what is the training most suitable for an analyst. My own view was and still remains that it is not the training prescribed by the University for future doctors. What is known as medical education appears to me to be an arduous and circuitous way of approaching the profession of analysis. No doubt it offers an analyst much that is indispensable to him. But it burdens him with too much else of which he can never make use, and there is a danger of its diverting his interest and his whole mode of thought from the understanding of psychical phenomena. A scheme of training for analysts has still to be created. It must include elements from the mental sciences, from psychology, the history of civilization and sociology, as well as from anatomy, biology and the study of evolution. There is so much to be taught in all this that it is justifiable to omit from the curriculum anything which has no direct bearing on the practice of analysis and only serves indirectly (like any other study) as a training for the intellect and for the powers of observation. It is easy to meet this suggestion by objecting that analytic colleges of this kind do not exist and that I am merely setting up an ideal. An ideal, no doubt. But an ideal which can and must be realized. And in our training institutes, in spite of all their youthful insufficiencies, that realization has already begun.

It will not have escaped my readers that in what I have said I have assumed as axiomatic something that is still violently disputed in the discussion. I have assumed, that is to say, that psycho-analysis is not a specialized branch of medicine. I cannot see how it is possible to dispute this. Psycho-analysis is a part of psychology; not of medical psychology in the old sense, not of the psychology of morbid processes, but simply of psychology. It is certainly not the whole of psychology, but its substructure and perhaps even its entire foundation. The possibility of its application to medical purposes must not lead us astray. Electricity and radiology also have their medical application, but the science to which they both belong is none the less physics. Nor can their situation be affected by historical arguments. The whole theory of electricity had its origin in an observation of a nerve-muscle preparation; yet no one would dream to-day of regarding it as a part of physiology. It is argued that psycho-analysis was after all discovered by a physician in the course of his efforts to assist his patients. But that is clearly neither here nor there. Moreover, the historical argument is double-edged. We might pursue the story and recall the unfriendliness and indeed the animosity with which the medical profession treated analysis from the very first. That would seem to imply that it can have no claims over analysis to-day. And though I do not accept that implication, I still feel some doubts as to whether the present wooing of psycho-analysis by the doctors is based, from the point of view of the libido theory, upon the first or upon the second of Abraham's sub-stages[1]—whether they wish to take possession of their object for the purpose of destroying or of preserving it.

I should like to consider the historical argument a moment longer. Since it is with me personally that we are concerned, I can throw a little light, for anyone who may be interested, on my own motives. After forty-one years of medical activity, my self-knowledge tells me that I have never really been a doctor in the proper sense. I became a doctor through being compelled to deviate from my original purpose; and the triumph of my life lies in my having, after a long and roundabout journey, found my way back to my earliest path. I have no knowledge of having had any craving in my early childhood to help suffering humanity. My innate sadistic disposition was not a very strong one, so that I had no need to develop this one of its derivatives. Nor did I ever play the 'doctor game'; my infantile curiosity evidently chose other paths. In my youth I felt an overpowering need to understand something of the riddles of the world in which we live and perhaps even to contribute something to their solution. The most hopeful means of achieving this end seemed to be to enrol myself in the medical faculty; but even after that I experimented—unsuccessfully—with zoology and chemistry, till at last, under the influence of Brücke,[2] who carried more weight with me than anyone else in my whole life, I settled down to physiology, though in those

---

[1][Abraham supposed that the oral stage of a child's libidinal development included a first, or sucking, sub-stage in which it had no hostile feelings towards its object (the breast) and a second, or biting, sub-stage, in which it destroyed its object as it incorporated it.]

[2][Ernst Wilhelm von Brücke (1819–92), head of the Vienna Institute of Physiology, in which Freud began his scientific career.]

days it was too narrowly restricted to histology. By that time
I had already passed all my medical examinations; but I took
no interest in anything to do with medicine till the teacher
whom I so deeply respected warned me that in view of my
impoverished material circumstances I could not possibly
take up a theoretical career. Thus I passed from the histology of the nervous system to neuropathology and then,
prompted by fresh influences, I began to be concerned with
the neuroses. I scarcely think, however, that my lack of a
genuine medical temperament has done much damage to
my patients. For it is not greatly to the advantage of patients
if their doctor's therapeutic interest has too marked an emotional emphasis. They are best helped if he carries out his
task coolly and keeping as close as possible to the rules.

No doubt what I have just said throws little light on the
problem of lay analysis; but it was only intended to exhibit
my personal credentials as being myself a supporter of the
inherent value of psycho-analysis and of its independence of
its application to medicine. But it will be objected at this
point that whether psycho-analysis, regarded as a science, is
a subdivision of medicine or of psychology is a purely academic question and of no practical interest. The real point
at issue, it will be said, is a different one, namely the application of analysis to the treatment of patients; in so far as it
claims to do this it must be content, the argument will run,
to be accepted as a specialized branch of medicine, like
radiology, for instance, and to submit to the rules laid down
for all therapeutic methods. I recognize that that is so; I
admit it. I only want to feel assured that the therapy will not
destroy the science. Unluckily analogies never carry one
more than a certain distance; a point is soon reached at
which the subjects of the comparison take divergent paths.
The case of analysis differs from that of radiology. A physicist does not require to have a patient in order to study the

laws that govern X-rays. But the only subject-matter of psycho-analysis is the mental processes of human beings and it is only in human beings that it can be studied. For reasons which can easily be understood, neurotic human beings offer far more instructive and accessible material than normal ones, and to withhold that material from anyone who wishes to study and apply analysis is to dock him of a good half of his training possibilities. I have, of course, no intention of asking that the interests of neurotic patients should be sacrificed to those of instruction and scientific research. The aim of my small volume on the question of lay analysis was precisely to show that, if certain precautions are observed, the two interests can quite easily be brought into harmony and that the interests of medicine, as rightly understood, will not be the last to profit by such a solution.

I myself brought forward all the necessary precautions and I can safely say that the discussion added nothing on this point. But I should like to remark that the emphasis was often placed in a manner which did not do justice to the facts. What was said about the difficulties of differential diagnosis and the uncertainty in many cases in deciding about somatic symptoms—situations, that is, in which medical knowledge and medical intervention are necessary—this is all of it perfectly true. Nevertheless, the number of cases in which doubts of this kind never arise at all and in which a doctor is *not* required is surely incomparably greater. These cases may be quite uninteresting scientifically, but they play an important enough part in life to justify the activity of lay analysts, who are perfectly competent to deal with them. Some time ago I analysed a colleague who gave evidence of a particularly strong dislike of the idea of anyone being allowed to engage in a medical activity who was not himself a medical man. I was in a position to say to him: 'We have now been working for more than three months. At what point in our analysis have I had occasion to make use of my medical knowledge?' He admitted that I had had no such occasion.

Again, I attach no great importance to the argument that a lay analyst, because he must be prepared to consult a doctor, will have no authority in the eyes of his patients and will be treated with no more respect than such people as bone-setters or masseurs. Once again, the analogy is an imperfect one—quite apart from the fact that what governs patients in their recognition of authority is usually their emotional transference and that the possession of a medical diploma does not impress them nearly so much as doctors believe. A professional lay analyst will have no difficulty in winning as much respect as is due to a secular pastoral worker. Indeed, the words, 'secular pastoral worker', might well serve as a general formula for describing the function which the analyst, whether he is a doctor or a layman, has to perform in his relation to the public. Our friends among the Protestant clergy, and more recently among the Catholic clergy as well, are often able to relieve their parishioners of the inhibitions of their daily life by confirming their faith—after having first offered them a little analytic information about the nature of their conflicts. Our opponents, the Adlerian 'Individual Psychologists', endeavour to produce a similar result in people who have become unstable and inefficient by arousing their interest in the social community—after having first thrown some light upon a single corner of their mental life and shown them the part played in their illness by their egoistic and distrustful impulses. Both of these procedures, which derive their power from being based on analysis, have their place in psychotherapy. We who are analysts set before us as our aim the most complete and profoundest possible analysis of whoever may be our patient. We do not seek to bring him relief by receiving him into the Catholic, Protestant or socialist community. We seek rather to enrich him from his own internal sources, by putting at the disposal of his ego those energies which, owing to repression, are inaccessibly confined in his unconscious, as well as those which his ego is obliged to squander in the fruitless task of maintaining these repressions. Such activity as this is pastoral work in the best sense of the words. Have we set ourselves too high an aim? Are the majority of our patients worth the pains that this work requires of us? Would it not be more economical to prop up their weaknesses from without rather than to rebuild them from within? I cannot say; but there is something else that I *do* know. In psycho-analysis there has existed from the very first an inseparable bond between cure and research. Knowledge brought therapeutic success. It was impossible to treat a patient without learning something new; it was impossible to gain fresh insight without perceiving its beneficent results. Our analytic procedure is the only one in which this precious conjunction is assured. It is only by carrying on our analytic pastoral work that we can deepen our dawning comprehension of the human mind. This prospect of scientific gain has been the proudest and happiest feature of analytic work. Are we to sacrifice it for the sake of any considerations of a practical sort?

Some remarks that have been made in the course of this discussion have led me to suspect that, in spite of everything, my book on lay analysis has been misunderstood in one respect. The doctors have been defended against me, as though I had declared that they were in general incompetent to practise analysis and as though I had given it out as a pass-word that medical reinforcements were to be rejected. That was far from my intention. The idea probably arose from my having been led to declare in the course of my observations (which had a controversial end in view) that untrained medical analysts were even more dangerous than laymen. I might make my true opinion on this question clear by echoing a cynical remark about women that once appeared in *Simplicissimus*. One man was complaining to another about the weaknesses and troublesome nature of the fair sex. 'All the same,' replied his companion, 'women are the best thing we have of the kind.' I am bound to admit that, so long as schools such as we desire for the training of analysts are not yet in existence, people who have had a preliminary education in medicine are the best material for future analysts. We have a right to demand, however, that they should not mistake their preliminary education for a complete training, that they should overcome the one-sidedness that is fostered by instruction in medical schools and that they should resist the temptation to flirt with endocrinology and the autonomic nervous system, when what is needed is an apprehension of psychological facts with the help of a framework of psychological concepts. I also share the view that all those problems which relate to the connection between psychical phenomena and their organic, anatomical and chemical foundations can be approached only by those who have studied both, that is, by medical analysts. It should not be forgotten, however, that this is not the whole of psycho-analysis, and that for its other aspect we can never do without the co-operation of people who have had a preliminary education in the *mental* sciences. For practical reasons we have been in the habit—and this is true, incidentally, of our publications as well—of distinguishing between medical and applied analysis. But that is not a logical distinction. The true line of division is between *scientific* analysis and its *applications* alike in medical and in non-medical fields.

In these discussions the bluntest rejection of lay analysis has been expressed by our American colleagues. A few words to them in reply will, I think, not be out of place. I can scarcely be accused of making a misuse of analysis for controversial purposes if I express an opinion that their resistance is derived wholly from practical factors. They see how in their own country lay analysts put analysis to all kinds of mischievous and illegitimate purposes and in consequence cause injury both to their patients and to the good name of analysis. It is therefore not to be wondered at if in their indignation they give the widest possible berth to such unscrupulous mischief-makers and try to prevent any layman from having a share in analysis. But these facts are already enough to diminish the significance of the American position; for the question of lay analysis must not be decided on practical considerations alone, and local conditions in America cannot be the sole determining influence on our views.

The resolution passed by our American colleagues against lay analysts, based as it essentially is upon practical reasons, appears to me nevertheless to be unpractical; for it cannot affect any of the factors which govern the situation. It is more or less equivalent to an attempt at repression. If it is impossible to prevent the lay analysts from pursuing their activities and if the public does not support the campaign against them, would it not be more expedient to recognize the fact of their existence by offering them opportunities for training? Might it not be possible in this way to gain some influence over them? And, if they were offered as an inducement the possibility of receiving the approval of the medical profession and of being invited to co-operate, might they not have some interest in raising their own ethical and intellectual level?

Vienna, June 1927.

INDEX

Introduction

*S*ince April 1956, millions of readers around the world
have found daily inspiration, hope, comfort, and biblical
truth from the pages of *Our Daily Bread*. Now you can find
inspiration and quiet moments for the Christmas season from
one of the most beloved devotionals, compiled into one conve-
nient volume.

We believe that this book will be of help to you and those
you know in every circumstance of life. May it and the Word of
God bring strength to your soul.

A Season of Renewal

Do you not know?
*   Have you not heard?*
The LORD is the everlasting God,
*   the Creator of the ends of the earth.*
He will not grow tired or weary,
*   and his understanding no one can fathom.*
He gives strength to the weary
*   and increases the power of the weak.*
Even youths grow tired and weary,
*   and young men stumble and fall;*
but those who hope in the LORD
*   will renew their strength.*
They will soar on wings like eagles;
*   they will run and not grow weary,*
*   they will walk and not be faint.*

—ISAIAH 40:28–31

A survey showed that 84 percent of people in the United States want a less materialistic holiday season. I suspect the same is true of people in many other countries. But when all roads seem to lead to the shopping malls, what is the pathway toward a more spiritual and meaningful celebration of Christ's birth?

Some church leaders are suggesting that we put more attention on the observance of Advent, the four-week period before Christmas. Instead of filling those days with activity and ending up physically and spiritually depleted, we need to recall that "those who hope in the LORD will renew their strength. They will soar on wings like eagles; they will run and not grow weary, they will walk and not be faint" (Isaiah 40:31).

Even with a busy calendar of school and church programs, and family obligations, we can still carve out time to "hope in the LORD" and to concentrate on the true meaning of this season. We can determine to make the most of our times of daily Bible reading and prayer, and to give *people* priority over *things*.

As we take time to focus on Christ's birth and to strengthen our relationship with Him, this time of year can become a season of renewal instead of exhaustion.   —DAVID MCCASLAND

The Gift of Joy

And there were shepherds living out in the fields nearby, keeping watch over their flocks at night. An angel of the LORD appeared to them, and the glory of the LORD shone around them, and they were terrified. But the angel said to them, "Do not be afraid. I bring you good news of great joy that will be for all the people. Today in the town of David a Savior has been born to you; he is Christ the LORD. This will be a sign to you: You will find a baby wrapped in cloths and lying in a manger." . . .

So they hurried off and found Mary and Joseph, and the baby, who was lying in the manger. When they had seen him, they spread the word concerning what had been told them about this child, and all who heard it were amazed at what the shepherds said to them. But Mary treasured up all these things and pondered them in her heart. The shepherds returned, glorifying and praising God for all the things they had heard and seen, which were just as they had been told. —LUKE 2:8–12, 16–20

*D*uring the Christmas season it's easy to be swept along by the flood of frenzied gift-buying. Our motive may be commendable—we want to show our love for family and friends. We may even argue that the exchange of expensive presents reflects God's gift to us of His Son and is a way to spread yuletide joy.

According to author Bill McKibben, though, we may be robbing ourselves and others of deeper and longer-lasting joy. When the giving is over, we find that the gifts didn't bring the sought-after satisfaction.

McKibben and some of his friends began to encourage others to limit their total holiday spending to a fraction of what they had spent in previous years. By taking the emphasis off gift-giving, they believe they will be able to concentrate more on the real reason for Christmas and to enjoy the season.

When the angel of the LORD appeared to the shepherds outside Bethlehem, he told them, "I bring you good news of great joy" (Luke 2:10). The news that brings "great joy" even today is that the Savior has been born (v. 11).

Have we lost sight of what's really at the heart of Christmas? Let's take time this season to focus on God's gift to us, and to share that joy-producing news with others.

—VERNON GROUNDS

O Holy Night

So Joseph also went up from the town of Nazareth in Galilee to Judea, to Bethlehem the town of David, because he belonged to the house and line of David. He went there to register with Mary, who was pledged to be married to him and was expecting a child. While they were there, the time came for the baby to be born, and she gave birth to her firstborn, a son. She wrapped him in cloths and placed him in a manger, because there was no room for them in the inn.

And there were shepherds living out in the fields nearby, keeping watch over their flocks at night. An angel of the LORD appeared to them, and the glory of the LORD shone around them, and they were terrified. But the angel said to them, "Do not be afraid. I bring you good news of great joy that will be for all the people. Today in the town of David a Savior has been born to you; he is Christ the LORD. This will be a sign to you: You will find a baby wrapped in cloths and lying in a manger."

Suddenly a great company of the heavenly host appeared with the angel, praising God and saying,

"Glory to God in the highest,
and on earth peace to men on whom his favor rests."

—LUKE 2:4–14

According to tradition, a Christmas song once brought peace to a battlefield. It happened on Christmas Eve during the Franco-German War (1870–1871) as the two sides faced each other in their trenches.

A French soldier jumped up and began singing "O Holy Night." The surprised German soldiers did not fire. Instead, one of them stepped forward to sing "From Heaven Above to Earth I Come."

For a brief time at least, peace on earth prevailed and good-will was shared among men whose job it was to kill each other.

Think about the words of "O Holy Night" and see how they can bring hostilities to a halt. "Long lay the world in sin and error pining." Who knows about the world's ills better than soldiers who are facing the consequences of war, killing, and death?

"A thrill of hope" is what those men needed in the darkness of that winter night. Hope is what "the dear Savior's birth" provides. Because of Him the "weary world rejoices."

Even though we may not be engaged in physical combat, we all face the battles of everyday life. We can let the peace of that holy night—the night of our dear Savior's birth—reign in our hearts the whole year through. —DAVE BRANON

The Shepherds

And there were shepherds living out in the fields nearby, keeping watch over their flocks at night. An angel of the LORD appeared to them, and the glory of the LORD shone around them, and they were terrified. But the angel said to them, "Do not be afraid. I bring you good news of great joy that will be for all the people."

—LUKE 2:8–10

The angel bypassed Jerusalem, the religious center of Israel. He didn't go to Herodium, Herod's villa near Bethlehem. He appeared instead to a band of shepherds tending their flocks (Luke 2:8–9).

Back then no one thought God would be interested in shepherds, or that shepherds would be interested in God. Shepherds were notoriously irreligious, ranked by the rabbis with prostitutes and other "habitual sinners." They were outcasts, barred from the synagogue and polite society. They assumed that God would never accept them, and they feared Him.

But God spoke to them. I think He knew that these shepherds, like so many people who appear indifferent to spiritual things, were quietly longing for God.

All of us have a longing for something more. And no matter how hard we try to appear self-sufficient, sooner or later we run out of something essential—love, money, time, or life. Isolation, loneliness, and fear of death lead us to acknowledge our need for a Savior. But where can we find Him?

The angel's words to the shepherds were simple and direct: "Today in the town of David a Savior has been born to you; he is Christ the LORD" (Luke 2:11). You can find Him too.

—DAVID ROPER

Something Happened Here

Through him all things were made; without him nothing was made that has been made. In him was life, and that life was the light of men. The light shines in the darkness, but the darkness has not understood it . . .

He was in the world, and though the world was made through him, the world did not recognize him. He came to that which was his own, but his own did not receive him. Yet to all who received him, to those who believed in his name, he gave the right to become children of God—children born not of natural descent, nor of human decision or a husband's will, but born of God.

The Word became flesh and made his dwelling among us. We have seen his glory, the glory of the One and Only, who came from the Father, full of grace and truth.   —JOHN 1:3–5, 10–14

*C*hristians are divided in their views of Christmas. Some want to give up on it and hand it over to the stores. Others want to salvage it and use it to say something important about the birth of Jesus to a weary secular world. I, for one, would like to take my place with the second group.

Years ago an old pioneer journeyed westward across the Great Plains of North America until he came to an abrupt halt at the edge of the Grand Canyon. He gawked at the sight before him—a vast chasm one mile deep, eighteen miles across, and stretching out of sight. He gasped, "Something must have happened here!"

At the Christmas season, anyone who stops to look and listen must ask what the hustle and bustle is all about. A thoughtful man or woman, seeing the lights, the decorations, the festivities, and the religious services might also conclude, "Something must have happened here!"

Of course, something did happen. We need to tell the world about it. God has visited our planet. His Son Jesus Christ came to reveal God and to die for our sins (John 1:1–14). It's the best news ever! The LORD came and lived among us that we might live forever with Him.

That's why we can rejoice at Christmas.

—HADDON ROBINSON

Weighed Down at Christmas

Jesus returned to Galilee in the power of the Spirit, and news about him spread through the whole countryside. He taught in their synagogues, and everyone praised him.

He went to Nazareth, where he had been brought up, and on the Sabbath day he went into the synagogue, as was his custom. And he stood up to read. The scroll of the prophet Isaiah was handed to him. Unrolling it, he found the place where it is written:

> "The Spirit of the LORD is on me,
> because he has anointed me
> to preach good news to the poor.
> He has sent me to proclaim freedom for the prisoners
> and recovery of sight for the blind,
> to release the oppressed,
> to proclaim the year of the LORD's favor."

Then he rolled up the scroll, gave it back to the attendant and sat down. The eyes of everyone in the synagogue were fastened on him, and he began by saying to them, "Today this scripture is fulfilled in your hearing."
—LUKE 4:14–21

$\mathcal{D}$uring a December visit to New York City's Metropolitan Museum of Art, I paused to admire the magnificent Christmas tree. It was covered with angels and surrounded at its base by an elaborate eighteenth-century nativity scene. Nearly two hundred figures, including shepherds, the Magi, and a crowd of townspeople, looked in anticipation toward the manger or gazed up in awe at the angels.

But one figure appeared different from the rest—a barefoot man, who carried a heavy load on his back and looked at the ground. It struck me that this man, like so many people today, was so weighed down that he couldn't see the Messiah.

Christmas can be a difficult time for those who carry the burden of hard work, stressful family situations, and personal loss. But we should remember that Christ came into our world to lift up all those who are bowed down. Jesus used the words of Isaiah to announce His God-given mission on earth: "To preach the gospel to the poor; . . . to heal the brokenhearted, to proclaim liberty to the captives and recovery of sight to the blind, to set at liberty those who are oppressed" (Luke 4:18 NKJV).

Jesus came to lift our burdens so we can raise our eyes to welcome Him at Christmas.　　　　　—DAVID MCCASLAND

The Child with Many Names

For to us a child is born,
to us a son is given,
and the government will be on his shoulders.
And he will be called
Wonderful Counselor, Mighty God,
Everlasting Father, Prince of Peace.

—ISAIAH 9:6

The Associated Press carried a story from England about a couple who gave their newborn daughter 139 names. They said they'll call her Tracy, but officially she'll be: Tracy Mariclaire Lisa Tammy Samantha Christine Alexandra . . . (you get the idea). When the father was asked why they did this, he said, "We just wanted to give her something for when she grows up." The article, carried by a local paper, was captioned, "What's In a Name? Don't Ask This Girl." Obviously her parents weren't thinking about the meaning of her names. They just wanted to do something unusual.

During this season we celebrate the birth of Jesus who also had many names. But in our LORD's case, all His titles are very significant. In biblical times, a person's name had great meaning; it did more than provide "a handle." It said something about the character of the person who bore it. That's especially important when we realize that Jesus is referred to in the Bible by many different titles each reflecting something about His person and work.

As Christians, we must make sure we know and experience Him in a manner consistent with His names. If we call Him "Jesus," which means "Savior," we must trust Him to deliver us from the power as well as the penalty of sin. If we call Him "LORD," we must allow Him to be just that. And what about such names as "Wonderful Counselor, Mighty God, Everlasting Father, Prince of Peace"? Do I act as if that's who He is?

—MART DE HAAN

Where's the Baby?

Again the LORD spoke to Ahaz, "Ask the LORD your God for a sign, whether in the deepest depths or in the highest heights."

But Ahaz said, "I will not ask; I will not put the LORD to the test."

Then Isaiah said, "Hear now, you house of David! Is it not enough to try the patience of men? Will you try the patience of my God also? Therefore the LORD himself will give you a sign: The virgin will be with child and will give birth to a son, and will call him Immanuel."   —ISAIAH 7:10–14

---

*T*wo women who were dressed in their finest were having lunch together in a very exclusive restaurant. A friend saw them and came over to their table to greet them. "What's the special occasion?" she asked. One of the women said, "We're having a birthday party for the baby in our family. He's two years old today." "But, where is the baby?" the friend asked. The child's mother answered, "Oh, I dropped him off at my mother's house. She's taking care of him until the party's over. It wouldn't have been any fun with him along."

How ridiculous—a birthday celebration for a child who wasn't welcome at his own party! Yet, when you stop to think about it, that's no more foolish than going through the Christmas season, with all of its festivities, without remembering the One whose birth we are supposed to be honoring.

And that's the way many people celebrate Christmas. In all the busyness—the party-going, gift-shopping, and family gatherings—the One whose birthday they are commemorating is almost completely forgotten.

As you move into this holiday season, in all of your good times with family and friends, make sure you don't leave out the LORD Jesus. Give Him the honor He deserves.

—RICHARD DE HAAN

Christmas Choice

After Jesus was born in Bethlehem in Judea, during the time of King Herod, Magi from the east came to Jerusalem and asked, "Where is the one who has been born king of the Jews? We saw his star in the east and have come to worship him."

When King Herod heard this he was disturbed, and all Jerusalem with him . . .

Herod called the Magi secretly and found out from them the exact time the star had appeared. He sent them to Bethlehem and said, "Go and make a careful search for the child. As soon as you find him, report to me, so that I too may go and worship him."

After they had heard the king, they went on their way, and the star they had seen in the east went ahead of them until it stopped over the place where the child was. When they saw the star, they were overjoyed. On coming to the house, they saw the child with his mother Mary, and they bowed down and worshiped him. Then they opened their treasures and presented him with gifts of gold and of incense and of myrrh. And having been warned in a dream not to go back to Herod, they returned to their country by another route.　　　　　　　　　　　—MATTHEW 2:1–3, 7–12

When Herod realized that he had been outwitted by the Magi, he was furious, and he gave orders to kill all the boys in Bethlehem and its vicinity who were two years old and under, in accordance with the time he had learned from the Magi.

The glitter of bright decorations, the sound of joyous Christmas carols, the happy children, and the cheerful "Merry Christmas" greetings sometimes give the impression that everybody is glad that Jesus came to our planet. But that isn't true today, and it never was.

The news of Jesus' birth evoked a mixed reaction. An angel brought "good tidings of great joy." The shepherds and wise men welcomed the Savior. But Herod was so troubled when he heard about it that he tried to destroy the baby Jesus. And the religious leaders of that day were indifferent. They sent no delegation to Bethlehem to find out what had happened.

Still today, thousands honor Jesus and rejoice in their salvation. But many others hate Him. They make efforts to outlaw the singing of Christmas carols in shopping malls and the display of nativity scenes in public places. Many others are apathetic. They go along with the celebration of the season. They join in singing Christmas carols. But they never ask themselves who Jesus is or why He came. They don't think of their responsibility to believe on Him and receive Him as their Savior.

Are you among the indifferent? To ignore Him and His claims is to reject Him. Christmas demands a decision about Christ. The choice is yours. —HERB VANDER LUGT

A Bad Christmas?

Mary got ready and hurried to a town in the hill country of Judea, where she entered Zechariah's home and greeted Elizabeth. When Elizabeth heard Mary's greeting, the baby leaped in her womb, and Elizabeth was filled with the Holy Spirit. In a loud voice she exclaimed: "Blessed are you among women, and blessed is the child you will bear! But why am I so favored, that the mother of my LORD should come to me? As soon as the sound of your greeting reached my ears, the baby in my womb leaped for joy. Blessed is she who has believed that what the LORD has said to her will be accomplished!" —LUKE 1:39–45

*J*ust about the time Americans have devoured the last Thanksgiving turkey leftovers, sad-faced TV newscasters tell them that it "looks like a bad Christmas" this year. What they mean is that sales in retail stores may be down during the upcoming Christmas buying season. And that makes for a "bad" Christmas.

Now, we understand why this is news. Many companies need a year-end consumer spending frenzy to stay afloat financially. Yet there's something in me that doesn't like people talking about a "bad" Christmas, even when it refers to poor retail sales. How can the celebration of the birth of the Messiah, the Savior of the world, ever be bad?

Let's look at that familiar story again. In the months before Jesus was born, Mary ventured to a nearby town to visit her relative Elizabeth, who also was expecting a child. As soon as Mary spoke, the baby in Elizabeth's womb leaped for joy. There was excitement in the air for those who knew the true identity of Mary's baby.

Let's recapture that joyous excitement by refocusing our attention on the event we celebrate rather than on the celebration of the event. It is Jesus' birth we are honoring, and that always makes for a good Christmas. —DAVE BRANON

The Big News

And there were shepherds living out in the fields nearby, keeping watch over their flocks at night. An angel of the LORD appeared to them, and the glory of the LORD shone around them, and they were terrified. But the angel said to them, "Do not be afraid. I bring you good news of great joy that will be for all the people. Today in the town of David a Savior has been born to you; he is Christ the LORD. This will be a sign to you: You will find a baby wrapped in cloths and lying in a manger."

Suddenly a great company of the heavenly host appeared with the angel, praising God and saying,

> *"Glory to God in the highest,*
> *and on earth peace to men on whom his favor rests."*

—LUKE 2:8–14

In December 1903, after many attempts, the Wright brothers were successful in getting their "flying machine" off the ground. Thrilled, they telegraphed this message to their sister Katherine: "We have actually flown 120 feet. Will be home for Christmas."

Katherine hurried to the editor of the local newspaper and showed him the message. He glanced at it and said, "How nice. The boys will be home for Christmas." He totally missed the big news—man had flown!

Many people today make a similar mistake when they hear the word Christmas. They don't think of Jesus and His miraculous birth. Instead, they think of family gatherings, festive meals, decorations, and gifts. To them, Christmas brings nostalgia and memories of childhood.

Now, all this celebration isn't wrong. But if that's all that Christmas means to us, we are missing its true significance. The true meaning of this special day is summed up in the words of the angel to the shepherds on that night long ago: "I bring you good news of great joy that will be for all the people. Today in the town of David a Savior has been born to you; he is Christ the LORD" (Luke 2:10–11).

That's the big news of Christmas!   —RICHARD DE HAAN

When God
Stepped Out

He is the image of the invisible God, the firstborn over all creation. For by him all things were created: things in heaven and on earth, visible and invisible, whether thrones or powers or rulers or authorities; all things were created by him and for him. He is before all things, and in him all things hold together. And he is the head of the body, the church; he is the beginning and the firstborn from among the dead, so that in everything he might have the supremacy. For God was pleased to have all his fullness dwell in him. —COLOSSIANS 1:15–19

We don't have to guess what God is like. Nor do we have to respond like the little boy who looked up at the sky and asked his mother, "Is God up there?" When she assured him that He was, the youngster replied, "Wouldn't it be nice if He would put His head out and let us see Him?"

What that boy didn't understand is that God did let us see Him. By sending His Son Jesus to earth, the heavenly Father fully revealed Himself as He is. Jesus was God "manifested in the flesh" (1 Timothy 3:16 NKJV). He made this clear when He said to Philip, "Anyone who has seen me has seen the Father" (John 14:9). Theologians refer to this truth as the incarnation.

This is the good news of Christmas: God has shown us what He is like in the person of His Son. He left heaven's glory and came down to earth to be born of a virgin. All the attributes of the infinite God resided in the Baby that Mary cradled in a Bethlehem manger. He was the "image of the invisible God," the One by whom "all things were created" and in whom "all things hold together" (Colossians 1:15–17).

As we pause to celebrate Jesus' birth, remember who He is. In Him we see displayed the holiness, the grace, and the love of the eternal God.

At Christmas, God did step out of heaven.

—PAUL VAN GORDER

An Unrecognized Gift

In those days Caesar Augustus issued a decree that a census should be taken of the entire Roman world. (This was the first census that took place while Quirinius was governor of Syria.) And everyone went to his own town to register.

So Joseph also went up from the town of Nazareth in Galilee to Judea, to Bethlehem the town of David, because he belonged to the house and line of David. He went there to register with Mary, who was pledged to be married to him and was expecting a child. While they were there, the time came for the baby to be born, and she gave birth to her firstborn, a son. She wrapped him in cloths and placed him in a manger, because there was no room for them in the inn.

—LUKE 2:1–7

*I*n the early nineteenth century, a war-weary world was anxiously watching the march of Napoleon. But during that time, obscure, seemingly insignificant events were occurring that would help to shape the future.

In 1809, between the battles of Trafalgar and Waterloo, William E. Gladstone was born in Liverpool; Alfred, Lord Tennyson in Summersby, England; Oliver Wendell Holmes in Boston; Felix Mendelssohn in Hamburg, Germany; and Abraham Lincoln in Hodgenville, Kentucky. Now, almost two hundred years later, is there the slightest doubt about the greater contribution to history—those battles or those babies?

So it was with the birth of Jesus. The Bethlehem crowd was all concerned about a census and the power of Rome. They had no inkling that the infinite infant Son of God was asleep in their little town. Only a few shepherds hurried to see Him who was born in a stable. And as they left, they glorified God.

We can get so caught up in the commercial busyness of this season that we overlook how great a gift this little Babe really was. Only when we remember that His sacrificial death for our sins and His resurrection from the grave were His destiny do we recognize His value to the human race. Then we can exclaim, "Thanks be to God for His indescribable gift!"

—DENNIS DE HAAN

The Main Event

The angel said to her, "Do not be afraid, Mary, you have found favor with God. You will be with child and give birth to a son, and you are to give him the name Jesus. He will be great and will be called the Son of the Most High. The LORD God will give him the throne of his father David, and he will reign over the house of Jacob forever; his kingdom will never end."

"How will this be," Mary asked the angel, "since I am a virgin?"

The angel answered, "The Holy Spirit will come upon you, and the power of the Most High will overshadow you. So the holy one to be born will be called the Son of God. Even Elizabeth your relative is going to have a child in her old age, and she who was said to be barren is in her sixth month. For nothing is impossible with God."

"I am the LORD's servant," Mary answered. "May it be to me as you have said." Then the angel left her. —LUKE 1:30–38

*D*uring the Great Depression that hit the United States in the 1930s, a family in the Midwest struggled to put food on their table. They had no money for luxuries.

One day, posters all over town announced that a circus was coming. Admission would be $1. A boy in the family wanted to see the show, but his father told him that he would have to earn the money on his own. The youngster had never seen a circus before, so he worked feverishly and was able to buy a ticket.

On the day the circus arrived, he went to see the performers and the animals parade through town. As he watched, a clown came dancing over to him, and the boy put his ticket in the clown's hand. Then he stood on the curb and cheered as the rest of the parade moved by.

The youngster rushed home to tell his parents what he had seen and how exciting the circus was. His father listened, then took his son in his arms and said, "Son, you didn't see the circus. All you saw was the parade."

That story is a parable of Christmas. Many people get excited about the festivities but miss the main event. During this season, let's remember what happened in a humble stable and what Jesus' birth means to us.   —HADDON ROBINSON

The Forgotten Tree

"We are witnesses of everything he did in the country of the Jews and in Jerusalem. They killed him by hanging him on a tree, but God raised him from the dead on the third day and caused him to be seen. He was not seen by all the people, but by witnesses whom God had already chosen—by us who ate and drank with him after he rose from the dead. He commanded us to preach to the people and to testify that he is the one whom God appointed as judge of the living and the dead. All the prophets testify about him that everyone who believes in him receives forgiveness of sins through his name."

—ACTS 10:39–43

*I*n Acts 10:39, the cross of Calvary is called a tree. It's also referred to this way in Acts 5:30, Acts 13:29, Galatians 3:13, and 1 Peter 2:24.

At this season when much attention is paid to the Christmas tree covered with tinsel, ornaments, and colored lights, the rugged cross of Calvary might well be called the forgotten tree of Christmas. Many people completely overlook the purpose for which Jesus came to earth. The true significance of His birth can be lost in the trappings, gift-giving, and party-going associated with the celebration of this holiday.

We must keep clearly in mind the real meaning of Christmas. Luke tells us that "the Son of Man came to seek and to save what was lost" (Luke 19:10). The Babe of Bethlehem was born to die. He came to give His life as a sacrifice for sin by hanging on a tree—not a tinsel-covered thing of beauty, but an ugly, cruel instrument of execution.

As we remember our Savior's birth in Bethlehem's stable, let's be deeply conscious that it is vitally related to Golgotha's hill where He was crucified, and where He shed His blood for the sins of the world.

Don't let Calvary's cross be the forgotten tree of Christmas. It's the most important one! —RICHARD DE HAAN

The Right Time?

Sons are a heritage from the LORD,
    children a reward from him.
Like arrows in the hands of a warrior
    are sons born in one's youth.
Blessed is the man
    whose quiver is full of them.
They will not be put to shame
    when they contend with their enemies in the gate.
Blessed are all who fear the LORD,
    who walk in his ways.
You will eat the fruit of your labor;
    blessings and prosperity will be yours.
Your wife will be like a fruitful vine
    within your house;
your sons will be like olive shoots
    around your table.
Thus is the man blessed
    who fears the LORD.

—PSALM 127:3–128:4

It was time. Not the time any of us would have chosen. Yet it was God's time. And we had gathered to accept it.

Specifically, it was the day in God's appointed timetable when my dad would be taken from us in death. His eighty-three good years of service to his Savior and his fifty-one loyal years of family leadership were over. His strong, determined body had at last succumbed to the relentless processes of aging and disease.

Yet it was Christmastime. The time of bright lights, joyous songs, and talk of Jesus' birth. It was time for anticipation, children's excitement, and peace on earth.

It was not a time, it would seem, to think about funeral arrangements and saying goodbye. How could this be the right time?

It was the right time because it was God's time. It was time for Dad to stop suffering. It was time for him to spend Christmas with Jesus. It was time for reunion with my sister in heaven—and how Dad liked reunions!

It was the right time because God never errs. He knew that my father's work was complete, his influence would live on, and his legacy was secure. He knew what He was doing. Dad was home for Christmas. It was time—God's time.

—DAVE BRANON

Wrapped Up in Greed

After they had heard the king, they went on their way, and the star they had seen in the east went ahead of them until it stopped over the place where the child was. When they saw the star, they were overjoyed. On coming to the house, they saw the child with his mother Mary, and they bowed down and worshiped him. Then they opened their treasures and presented him with gifts of gold and of incense and of myrrh. —MATTHEW 2:9–11

---

*A*s followers of Jesus, we must be careful to guard our hearts from greed during this holiday season. In a society that has secularized Christmas, that's not easy.

USA Today reported the results of three polls signaling the erosion of the meaning of Christmas. In a survey of Americans, only one-third said the birth of Jesus is what makes the holiday important.

What is important, then? The presents, of course! According to the poll, 97 percent of us purchase gifts.

While there's nothing wrong with commemorating the gift of God's Son by giving gifts to those we love, this pleasant tradition can easily become greed-infected. Remember the toy of choice in 1996, the Tickle Me Elmo doll? Some people bought one for a child or grandchild but gave up that loving idea after learning they could turn the toy into a big profit. Newspapers were soon carrying columns of ads offering the fad-of-the-season doll for many times its purchase price.

If you find yourself caught up in the greed of Christmas, take a moment to sit quietly. In your mind's eye, walk with the wise men to the Christ-child. Bow before Him and offer Him the gift of your love and worship. Instead of a greedy Christmas this year, let's make it a worshipful one. —DAVE EGNER

Sing a New Song

His father Zechariah was filled with the Holy Spirit and prophesied:

> "Praise be to the LORD, the God of Israel,
>> because he has come and has redeemed his people.
> He has raised up a horn of salvation for us
>> in the house of his servant David . . .
> And you, my child, will be called a prophet of the Most High;
>> for you will go on before the LORD to prepare the
>>> way for him,
> to give his people the knowledge of salvation
>> through the forgiveness of their sins,
> because of the tender mercy of our God,
>> by which the rising sun will come to us from heaven
> to shine on those living in darkness
>> and in the shadow of death,
> to guide our feet into the path of peace."

And the child grew and became strong in spirit; and he lived in the desert until he appeared publicly to Israel.

—LUKE 1:67–69, 76–80

*T*wo passages in Luke related to the birth of Jesus are often called "songs" because of their similarity to Hebrew psalms of the Old Testament. The early church set them to music and used them in worship. One of them, the Magnificat of Mary (1:46–55), is well known. But the second "song" is a less familiar poem of praise, which was spoken by Zacharias, the father of John the Baptist (vv. 67–79).

After nine months of divinely imposed silence, Zacharias was finally able to speak. He announced that the miracle baby born to him and Elizabeth would be named John. Then, filled with the Holy Spirit, Zacharias spoke of God's faithfulness and the salvation He would bring through Messiah.

Zacharias said that Jesus, "through the tender mercy of our God, with which the Dayspring from on high has visited us," would come "to give light to those who sit in darkness and the shadow of death, to guide our feet into the way of peace" (vv. 78–79).

For a fresh look at the birth of Jesus this Christmas, consider Zacharias' words of prophecy and exultation. Read them aloud. Ponder their meaning. Let God use them to write a new song of praise deep in your heart.   —DAVID MCCASLAND

The Spirit of Giving

This is how the birth of Jesus Christ came about: His mother Mary was pledged to be married to Joseph, but before they came together, she was found to be with child through the Holy Spirit. Because Joseph her husband was a righteous man and did not want to expose her to public disgrace, he had in mind to divorce her quietly.

But after he had considered this, an angel of the LORD appeared to him in a dream and said, "Joseph son of David, do not be afraid to take Mary home as your wife, because what is conceived in her is from the Holy Spirit. She will give birth to a son, and you are to give him the name Jesus, because he will save his people from their sins."

All this took place to fulfill what the LORD had said through the prophet: "The virgin will be with child and will give birth to a son, and they will call him Immanuel"—which means, "God with us."

When Joseph woke up, he did what the angel of the LORD had commanded him and took Mary home as his wife. But he had no union with her until she gave birth to a son. And he gave him the name Jesus.   —MATTHEW 1:18–25

Yes, there are people who believe in Santa Claus. According to a poll taken by KRC Research in 1996 and cited in *US News & World Report*, 9 percent of American adults say they really do believe in the jolly old North Pole resident.

Perhaps that's not surprising when we realize that at no other time of the year do we focus so much attention on a single theme as during the Christmas season. The fictional character of Santa Claus has become an integral part of the celebration in our culture because he symbolizes gift-giving, the centerpiece of most holiday gatherings. What many people believe in at Christmas is the spirit of giving.

As admirable as that spirit may be, there is something more grand and life-changing to believe in. At Christmas we need to focus on truths like these:

- The prophecies of Jesus' birth (Isaiah 7:14; 9:1–7).
- The miracle of Jesus' conception (Matthew 1:18).
- The perfection of the holy Christ-child (Luke 1:35).
- The mission of that baby boy (Matthew 1:21).

The Creator of the world miraculously became man on that first Christmas morning so He could provide us with the gift of eternal life. Now, that's something to believe in at Christmas!

—DAVE BRANON

A Witness at Christmas

What, then, was the purpose of the law? It was added because of transgressions until the Seed to whom the promise referred had come. The law was put into effect through angels by a mediator. A mediator, however, does not represent just one party; but God is one.

Is the law, therefore, opposed to the promises of God? Absolutely not! For if a law had been given that could impart life, then righteousness would certainly have come by the law. But the Scripture declares that the whole world is a prisoner of sin, so that what was promised, being given through faith in Jesus Christ, might be given to those who believe.

Before this faith came, we were held prisoners by the law, locked up until faith should be revealed. So the law was put in charge to lead us to Christ that we might be justified by faith. Now that faith has come, we are no longer under the supervision of the law.

—GALATIANS 3:19–25

*D*uring the holiday season, an atheistic organization put a sign alongside the community Christmas display in Madison, Wisconsin. It blatantly declared: "In this season of the winter solstice, may reason prevail. There are no gods, no devils, no angels, no heaven or hell. There is only our material world. Religion is but a myth and superstition that hardens hearts and enslaves minds."

On the back of that sign was the warning: Thou Shalt Not Steal. That warning, of course, is one of the Ten Commandments. How ironic that people who don't believe in God's existence would use one of His laws to keep someone from taking their sign! If there isn't any God to establish what is right and what is wrong, that commandment is a human directive that carries no authority.

The LORD gave the commandments to show us our sinfulness and need of forgiveness (Galatians 3:24). He then came into our world at Bethlehem in the person of Jesus so that we might be justified by faith in Him. That Christmas display and the words on the back of the protesters' sign bear testimony to our Savior's birth and to our need for Him.

Thank God for being the Lawgiver who came to earth to redeem the lawbreakers. —VERNON GROUNDS

The Baby Grew Up

This is how the birth of Jesus Christ came about: His mother Mary was pledged to be married to Joseph, but before they came together, she was found to be with child through the Holy Spirit. Because Joseph her husband was a righteous man and did not want to expose her to public disgrace, he had in mind to divorce her quietly.

But after he had considered this, an angel of the LORD appeared to him in a dream and said, "Joseph son of David, do not be afraid to take Mary home as your wife, because what is conceived in her is from the Holy Spirit. She will give birth to a son, and you are to give him the name Jesus, because he will save his people from their sins."

All this took place to fulfill what the LORD had said through the prophet: "The virgin will be with child and will give birth to a son, and they will call him Immanuel"—which means, "God with us."

When Joseph woke up, he did what the angel of the LORD had commanded him and took Mary home as his wife. But he had no union with her until she gave birth to a son. And he gave him the name Jesus.

—MATTHEW 1:18–25

*E*ven Christians can miss the point of the Christmas story if they aren't careful. Halford E. Luccock warned of that danger in a thought-provoking essay. He wrote: "We can become so charmed with the story of a baby that we grow sentimental about it. It does not ask that we do anything about it; it does not demand any vital change in our way of thinking and living.

"The great question for us is this: Is our Christmas still only a story about a baby, or is it more, a deathless story about a Person into whom the baby grew, who can redeem the world from its sins, and who calls us into partnership with His great and mighty purposes?"

When the angel of the LORD appeared to Joseph, he said, "You are to give him the name Jesus, because he will save his people from their sins" (Matthew 1:21). It is only as we see the birth of Jesus in light of His crucifixion and resurrection that we are able to grasp the full meaning of Christ's coming.

With your eyes wide open this Christmas, respond to God with love and commitment for the gift of His Son. Focus your thoughts and actions and motivations toward honoring the Baby who grew up and died for all our sins.

Christ the Savior is born!   —DAVID McCASLAND

Wishing on Stars

After Jesus was born in Bethlehem in Judea, during the time of King Herod, Magi from the east came to Jerusalem and asked, "Where is the one who has been born king of the Jews? We saw his star in the east and have come to worship him."...

They went on their way, and the star they had seen in the east went ahead of them until it stopped over the place where the child was. When they saw the star, they were overjoyed.

—MATTHEW 2:1–2, 9–10

On the night Jesus was born, the bright light of a single star announced His birth. It was an announcement that many had hoped and prayed for, yet many missed.

Perhaps they were like me. Perhaps their hopes were more like dreams and their prayers were more like wishes. Maybe they were looking for a star that would grant every whim, not a light that would reveal their sin.

Every Christmas when I sing in our church's annual Festival of Lights program, I wish for several things. I wish for those few magic moments when the choir is so perfectly in tune that I can't hear anyone, yet I can hear everyone. I think that's what the music of heaven will be like.

Every night when people are laughing at the drama, I wish that I could see what's so funny. But I always get stuck in a part of the choir loft that's behind the set.

Yes, I wish for these things, but I know that instead of wishing to hear the pure strains of a few songs, I ought to pray that I will hear God when He speaks.

Instead of wishing I could see the drama, I should pray that my eyes would see Jesus and not be distracted by the world.

Wishing is hoping I'll get what I want from God. A prayer is a plea that God will get what He wants from me.

—Julie Ackerman Link

What If?

Marshal your troops, O city of troops,
*   for a siege is laid against us.*
They will strike Israel's ruler
*   on the cheek with a rod.*
"But you, Bethlehem Ephrathah,
*   though you are small among the clans of Judah,*
out of you will come for me
*   one who will be ruler over Israel,*
whose origins are from of old,
*   from ancient times."*
Therefore Israel will be abandoned
*   until the time when she who is in labor gives birth*
and the rest of his brothers return
*   to join the Israelites.*
He will stand and shepherd his flock
*   in the strength of the LORD,*
*   in the majesty of the name of the LORD his God.*
And they will live securely, for then his greatness
*   will reach to the ends of the earth.*
*   And he will be their peace.*

—MICAH 5:1–5

*S*everal years ago a group of historians authored a book called *If—Or History Rewritten*. Some of the ifs those scholars considered were these: What if Robert E. Lee had not lost the Battle of Gettysburg? What if the Moors in Spain had won? What if the Dutch had kept New Amsterdam? What if Booth had missed when he shot at Abraham Lincoln? What if Napoleon had escaped to America?

The attempt to reconstruct the past on the basis of these *ifs* was only a historian's game. But apply it for a moment to the central event in history—the birth of Jesus Christ. It was foretold with pinpoint accuracy hundreds of years before by the prophet Micah. The greatest *if*, therefore—the most startling question to the imagination—is "What if Jesus had not been born as predicted?"

Such an if staggers the mind. It is like imagining the earth without a sunrise or the heavens without stars. Yet this if must be taken seriously, especially at Christmas, because our world is oblivious to the true meaning of Christ's coming.

Can you imagine what the world would be like without Christ? What would history have been without Him? And at a personal level, what would your life be without Him? Thank God that there are no *ifs* in history.   —HADDON ROBINSON

A Wonderful Life

You are all sons of God through faith in Christ Jesus, for all of you who were baptized into Christ have clothed yourselves with Christ. There is neither Jew nor Greek, slave nor free, male nor female, for you are all one in Christ Jesus. If you belong to Christ, then you are Abraham's seed, and heirs according to the promise.

What I am saying is that as long as the heir is a child, he is no different from a slave, although he owns the whole estate. He is subject to guardians and trustees until the time set by his father. So also, when we were children, we were in slavery under the basic principles of the world. But when the time had fully come, God sent his Son, born of a woman, born under law, to redeem those under law, that we might receive the full rights of sons. Because you are sons, God sent the Spirit of his Son into our hearts, the Spirit who calls out, "Abba, Father." So you are no longer a slave, but a son; and since you are a son, God has made you also an heir.
—GALATIANS 3:26–4:7

*E*ach December, millions of people around the world watch Frank Capra's 1946 film *It's A Wonderful Life*. Although it wasn't a hit when it debuted, it has become a Christmas classic.

In a *Time* magazine essay, Roger Rosenblatt pondered the film's continuing appeal. He concluded that the story is really about friendship. That helps to explain why we often feel choked up as we watch George Bailey's family and friends rally around him in his time of greatest need. Rosenblatt said, "Just when George thinks he's alone in the world, the world shows up to declare its love for him."

That sentence seems to capture the essence of our celebration of the birth of Jesus. Just when we thought we were alone in the world, Christ came to declare God's love for us. Not only did God send His Son into the world at exactly the right time (Galatians 4:4–5), but He also demonstrated "his own love for us in this: While we were still sinners, Christ died for us" (Romans 5:8). That's the message of Christmas that opens the door to a wonderful life—the joy of knowing Christ and living in His love.

Have you received the gift of eternal life that He offers to you? If not, do so today.　　　—DAVID MCCASLAND

Celebrate the Baby

And there were shepherds living out in the fields nearby, keeping watch over their flocks at night. An angel of the LORD appeared to them, and the glory of the LORD shone around them, and they were terrified. But the angel said to them, "Do not be afraid. I bring you good news of great joy that will be for all the people. Today in the town of David a Savior has been born to you; he is Christ the LORD. This will be a sign to you: You will find a baby wrapped in cloths and lying in a manger."

Suddenly a great company of the heavenly host appeared with the angel, praising God and saying,

> *"Glory to God in the highest,*
>   *and on earth peace to men on whom his favor rests."*

—LUKE 2:8–14

*W*hy do we celebrate Jesus' birthday so differently from other birthdays? When it's time to honor historical figures who have a day set aside for them, we don't think about them as babies. We don't have pictures of cute little Abe Lincoln in his log cabin in Kentucky. No, we remember him for his contributions as an adult.

It is proper, though, that we celebrate Jesus as a child. Think about it. When He was born, shepherds came to honor Him (Luke 2:15–16). Later, wise men from the East brought Him gifts (Matthew 2:8–12). These people had no idea what Christ would eventually accomplish as an adult. But they were right in doing what they did, because Jesus' birth was the most remarkable event in human history.

How amazing! God in human form. The Creator of the universe visiting this planet. Let's never hesitate to celebrate this baby at Christmas. Marvel at His incarnation. Stand in awe of the tiny baby who had created His worshipers. Then step back in wonder, for the story gets even better. This baby grew into manhood, lived a perfect life, and willingly died for your sins and mine.

Celebrate the baby and trust the Savior. That's how to make Christmas complete.   —DAVE BRANON

Hiding in Plain Sight

In the sixth month, God sent the angel Gabriel to Nazareth, a town in Galilee, to a virgin pledged to be married to a man named Joseph, a descendant of David. The virgin's name was Mary. The angel went to her and said, "Greetings, you who are highly favored! The LORD is with you."

Mary was greatly troubled at his words and wondered what kind of greeting this might be. But the angel said to her, "Do not be afraid, Mary, you have found favor with God. You will be with child and give birth to a son, and you are to give him the name Jesus. He will be great and will be called the Son of the Most High. The LORD God will give him the throne of his father David, and he will reign over the house of Jacob forever; his kingdom will never end."

"How will this be," Mary asked the angel, "since I am a virgin?" The angel answered, "The Holy Spirit will come upon you, and the power of the Most High will overshadow you. So the holy one to be born will be called the Son of God.

—LUKE 1:26–35

Baltimore congregation found the answer to their financial troubles on the wall of their church. And it had been "hiding" there for more than twenty-five years! Someone finally recognized a piece of art hanging in the chapel—it was a valuable woodblock print by Albrecht Dürer, dated 1493. The work shows the angel telling Mary she would give birth to God's Son.

Some members just could not believe they had been unaware of the value of the old masterpiece, saying in effect, "If it were real, why would it be here?"

What about us? Are we overlooking the value of the event depicted on that woodblock print?

Jesus isn't hiding. The truth that God came to earth in human form is plainly announced in His Word. It is reflected in our art and in our hymnbooks. But the significance of Christ's birth is still neglected. We get so wrapped up in activities and programs that we miss the immeasurable worth of knowing who that Baby was.

What's missing is our worship. Think about the meaning of His birth. Jesus is God! He came to save us from our sins (Matthew 1:21) and give us eternal life (John 3:14–18).

This Christmas, join with the wisemen and shepherds and give praise to Jesus—God who became Man.

—MART DE HAAN

Letdown

Suddenly a great company of the heavenly host appeared with the angel, praising God and saying,

"Glory to God in the highest,
    and on earth peace to men on whom his favor rests."

When the angels had left them and gone into heaven, the shepherds said to one another, "Let's go to Bethlehem and see this thing that has happened, which the LORD has told us about."

So they hurried off and found Mary and Joseph, and the baby, who was lying in the manger. When they had seen him, they spread the word concerning what had been told them about this child, and all who heard it were amazed at what the shepherds said to them. But Mary treasured up all these things and pondered them in her heart. The shepherds returned, glorifying and praising God for all the things they had heard and seen, which were just as they had been told. —LUKE 2:13–20

The night of Jesus' birth was exciting for Mary and Joseph. There before their eyes was the miracle Baby whose coming into the world had been announced by an angel. The shepherds too were excited when they saw and heard "a multitude of the heavenly host praising God" and heralding His birth (Luke 2:13 NKJV).

But it wouldn't be long before Mary and Joseph would face the ordinary tasks of caring for a new baby and all the accompanying responsibilities. The shepherds would be back on the hillside tending their sheep. All the elements were in place for an emotional letdown, which often follows an emotional high.

I don't believe they experienced any "after-Christmas blues," however. Mary didn't quickly forget all that had happened, and the shepherds couldn't easily forget what they had heard and seen (vv. 19–20). The angelic message had proven true, and their lives were filled with new hope and anticipation.

There's no reason for an after-Christmas letdown. We have the full story. Jesus came to die for our sins, and then conquered death for us by rising from the grave. We have more truth to ponder and more reason to glorify God than Mary and the shepherds did. —HERB VANDER LUGT

The Place of Going Forth

Marshal your troops, O city of troops,
   for a siege is laid against us.
They will strike Israel's ruler
   on the cheek with a rod.
"But you, Bethlehem Ephrathah,
   though you are small among the clans of Judah,
out of you will come for me
   one who will be ruler over Israel,
whose origins are from of old,
   from ancient times."
Therefore Israel will be abandoned
   until the time when she who is in labor gives birth
and the rest of his brothers return
   to join the Israelites.
He will stand and shepherd his flock
   in the strength of the LORD,
   in the majesty of the name of the LORD his God.
And they will live securely, for then his greatness
   will reach to the ends of the earth.

—MICAH 5:1–4

A lot of attention was suddenly focused on the small town of Bethlehem. Jews from many parts of the world came to be counted in a census. Mary and Joseph traveled there from Nazareth. Shepherds came from the fields to see the Baby lying in a manger (Luke 2:15–16) after a multitude of angels had come to announce, "Glory to God in the highest, and on earth peace to men on whom his favor rests" (vv. 13–14).

Every Christmas, in our imagination we go to Bethlehem to celebrate Jesus' birth. But we cannot stay there; we must leave. The angels returned to heaven. Mary and Joseph went to Jerusalem, and then sought safety in Egypt.

The shepherds' exit gives a clear message to us. They left the stable and told everyone about the holy Child. "And all who heard it were amazed at what the shepherds said to them" (v. 18).

It's appropriate for us to do the same. Micah prophesied that from Bethlehem would go forth a Ruler of Israel, the eternal Maker of the world, who had come to save mankind from sin (Micah 5:2). This season, let's join those who have gone forth from their visits to Bethlehem to proclaim the good news of Christ, who came to save us. —DAVE EGNER

A Fitting Present

On coming to the house, they saw the child with his mother Mary, and they bowed down and worshiped him. Then they opened their treasures and presented him with gifts of gold and of incense and of myrrh. And having been warned in a dream not to go back to Herod, they returned to their country by another route.

When they had gone, an angel of the LORD appeared to Joseph in a dream. "Get up," he said, "take the child and his mother and escape to Egypt. Stay there until I tell you, for Herod is going to search for the child to kill him." So he got up, took the child and his mother during the night and left for Egypt, where he stayed until the death of Herod. And so was fulfilled what the LORD had said through the prophet: "Out of Egypt I called my son."

—MATTHEW 2:11–15

A little boy was somewhat perplexed by all the exchanging of presents on Christmas morning, for he had been taught in Sunday school that it was the birthday of the Savior. Finally, after a long period of silence, he asked, "Mommy, when are we going to give Jesus His present? I thought it was His birthday!"

Strange, isn't it, that most of us give gifts to everyone but the One whose birthday we celebrate. A good question we might ask ourselves is this: What am I going to give to the LORD Jesus this Christmas? If you have never trusted in Him as your Savior, the thing He desires most from you is a believing heart. Why not put your faith in Jesus' sacrificial death on the cross so you can be saved from your sins?

If by faith you already know Christ as your Savior, then the most wonderful thing you can do this Christmas is to present to God the one gift He most desires to receive from you—your body (Romans 12:1).

Our bodies are to be used for God's purposes. Because we have accepted the gift of salvation from Him, it's only reasonable that we should present ourselves to the Father. When we give ourselves, we give the one Christmas present that truly fits the occasion!   —RICHARD DE HAAN

A Christmas Rose

This is how the birth of Jesus Christ came about: His mother Mary was pledged to be married to Joseph, but before they came together, she was found to be with child through the Holy Spirit. Because Joseph her husband was a righteous man and did not want to expose her to public disgrace, he had in mind to divorce her quietly.

But after he had considered this, an angel of the LORD appeared to him in a dream and said, "Joseph son of David, do not be afraid to take Mary home as your wife, because what is conceived in her is from the Holy Spirit. She will give birth to a son, and you are to give him the name Jesus, because he will save his people from their sins."

All this took place to fulfill what the LORD had said through the prophet: "The virgin will be with child and will give birth to a son, and they will call him Immanuel"—which means, "God with us."

When Joseph woke up, he did what the angel of the LORD had commanded him and took Mary home as his wife. But he had no union with her until she gave birth to a son. And he gave him the name Jesus.

—MATTHEW 1:18–25

*I*n contrast to many of the resounding carols proclaiming the Savior's birth, "Lo, How A Rose E'er Blooming" is a gentle song. Written in the fifteenth century by an unknown German poet, it stands quietly in the midst of our modern Christmas rush, bearing a message of joy for all who will pause to listen.

> *Lo, how a Rose e'er blooming*
> *From tender stem hath sprung!*
> *Of Jesse's lineage coming,*
> *As men of old have sung.*
> *It came, a floweret bright,*
> *Amid the cold of winter,*
> *When half spent was the night.*

The song speaks of a season when roses don't bloom and of a night half gone, a time when people often give in to despair.

Christmas can be an emotional winter, a dark night when the holiday lights are dimmed and cheery greetings are muted by loneliness or fear. Yet there is this word of hope:

> *This Flower, whose fragrance tender*
> *With sweetness fills the air,*
> *Dispels with glorious splendor*
> *The darkness everywhere;*
> *True man, yet very God,*
> *From sin and death He saves us,*
> *And lightens every load.*

A Rose has bloomed at midnight in winter. Christ the Savior is born!
— David McCasland

A Promise Fulfilled

This is how the birth of Jesus Christ came about: His mother Mary was pledged to be married to Joseph, but before they came together, she was found to be with child through the Holy Spirit. Because Joseph her husband was a righteous man and did not want to expose her to public disgrace, he had in mind to divorce her quietly.

But after he had considered this, an angel of the LORD appeared to him in a dream and said, "Joseph son of David, do not be afraid to take Mary home as your wife, because what is conceived in her is from the Holy Spirit. She will give birth to a son, and you are to give him the name Jesus, because he will save his people from their sins."

All this took place to fulfill what the LORD had said through the prophet: "The virgin will be with child and will give birth to a son, and they will call him Immanuel"—which means, "God with us."

When Joseph woke up, he did what the angel of the LORD had commanded him and took Mary home as his wife. But he had no union with her until she gave birth to a son. And he gave him the name Jesus.
                                                    —MATTHEW 1:18–25

In the off-season of baseball, managers and coaches concentrate on trading players to set themselves up for a winning season the next year. But if you are a Chicago Cubs fan like I am, you don't expect much because we haven't won a championship in years! That made the promise from a newly acquired player for the Cubs sound rather incredible. To a packed press conference, he said, "We are going to win the World Series!" I have to admit, it was hard not to be skeptical. It sounded like a promise that most likely he couldn't deliver.

No doubt the Jews of Jesus' day who were living under the oppressive thumb of Rome had to wonder if God would ever make good on His promise to send a Deliverer who would forgive sin and restore the glory of Israel (Isaiah 1:26; 53:12; 61). God had long ago promised one, but they hadn't heard a word from Him in four hundred years. But then, at just the right moment, the angel announced to Joseph that Mary would give birth to a Son who would "save His people from their sins" (Matthew 1:21).

Christmas proves that God is a promise-keeping God! He said that He would send a Deliverer, and He did. Your sin is not beyond the reach of this promise. He is ready and waiting to forgive your sins—all of them. —JOE STOWELL

Blue Christmas

Who has believed our message
   and to whom has the arm of the LORD been revealed?
He grew up before him like a tender shoot,
   and like a root out of dry ground.
He had no beauty or majesty to attract us to him,
   nothing in his appearance that we should desire him.
He was despised and rejected by men,
   a man of sorrows, and familiar with suffering.
Like one from whom men hide their faces
   he was despised, and we esteemed him not.
Surely he took up our infirmities
   and carried our sorrows,
yet we considered him stricken by God,
   smitten by him, and afflicted.
But he was pierced for our transgressions,
   he was crushed for our iniquities;
the punishment that brought us peace was upon him,
   and by his wounds we are healed.
We all, like sheep, have gone astray,
   each of us has turned to his own way;
and the LORD has laid on him
   the iniquity of us all.

—ISAIAH 53:1–6

A growing number of churches are holding annual Blue Christmas services for those faced with grief and loss. The holiday season's emphasis on happiness and good cheer often makes people who are dealing with heartbreak feel even worse.

An Associated Press article quoted a pastor who described the Blue Christmas service as "an opportunity for people to come and be in the presence of God and acknowledge their grief and despair and loneliness and give it to God." One participant added, "And it's a good place to have a cry and no one will mind."

During the Christmas season, we often read Isaiah's prophecies of the coming Messiah who would be born of a virgin (Isaiah 7:14) and called "Wonderful Counselor, Mighty God, Everlasting Father, Prince of Peace" (9:6). But perhaps we should also include the words of Isaiah 53: "He was . . . a man of sorrows and familiar with suffering . . . Surely he took up our infirmities and carried our sorrows . . . And by his wounds we are healed" (vv. 3–5). The psalmist reminds us that "[The LORD] heals the brokenhearted and binds up their wounds" (Psalm 147:3).

If you're hurting this Christmas, remember: Jesus came to save us, to help us, and to heal us.   —DAVID MCCASLAND

Reserved in Heaven

Praise be to the God and Father of our LORD Jesus Christ! In his great mercy he has given us new birth into a living hope through the resurrection of Jesus Christ from the dead, and into an inheritance that can never perish, spoil or fade—kept in heaven for you, who through faith are shielded by God's power until the coming of the salvation that is ready to be revealed in the last time. In this you greatly rejoice, though now for a little while you may have had to suffer grief in all kinds of trials. These have come so that your faith—of greater worth than gold, which perishes even though refined by fire—may be proved genuine and may result in praise, glory and honor when Jesus Christ is revealed. Though you have not seen him, you love him; and even though you do not see him now, you believe in him and are filled with an inexpressible and glorious joy, for you are receiving the goal of your faith, the salvation of your souls. —I PETER 1:3–9

A friend of mine spent several months rebuilding an old Ford Bronco and turning it into an off-road vehicle for use here in Idaho. He kept it in his garage under lock and key. When Christmas came, Gary thought, "What better place to hide my daughter Katie's present."

Shortly before Christmas, someone asked Katie what she was getting for Christmas. "Oh," she replied, "I already have it. It's a bicycle in a box under the Bronco in the garage!"

I don't know what methods Katie used to discover her present. But I do admire her unshakable confidence that the bike was hers even though she did not yet have it in her hands.

That confidence reminds me of the apostle Peter's words: "[God] has given us new birth into a living hope through the resurrection of Jesus Christ from the dead, and into an inheritance that can never perish, spoil or fade—kept in heaven for you, who through faith are shielded by God's power until the coming of the salvation that is ready to be revealed in the last time" (1 Peter 1:3–5).

What is reserved for us? Our inheritance—heaven, and a legacy beyond description that rests on the certainty of eternal life, "which God, who does not lie, promised before the beginning of time" (Titus 1:2).   —DAVID ROPER

The Forgotten Man

This is how the birth of Jesus Christ came about: His mother Mary was pledged to be married to Joseph, but before they came together, she was found to be with child through the Holy Spirit. Because Joseph her husband was a righteous man and did not want to expose her to public disgrace, he had in mind to divorce her quietly.

But after he had considered this, an angel of the LORD appeared to him in a dream and said, "Joseph son of David, do not be afraid to take Mary home as your wife, because what is conceived in her is from the Holy Spirit. She will give birth to a son, and you are to give him the name Jesus, because he will save his people from their sins."

All this took place to fulfill what the LORD had said through the prophet: "The virgin will be with child and will give birth to a son, and they will call him Immanuel"—which means, "God with us."

When Joseph woke up, he did what the angel of the LORD had commanded him and took Mary home as his wife. But he had no union with her until she gave birth to a son. And he gave him the name Jesus.   —MATTHEW 1:18–25

$\mathscr{A}$mid all the Christmas activities, one man is often for-gotten.

No, I don't mean the person whose birthday we're celebrat-ing. Although we often fail to give Jesus first place as He deserves, we don't usually forget Him. I'm talking about Joseph—the man God trusted so much that He placed His Son in his home to love and nurture. What a responsibility!

Joseph truly is the forgotten man in the Christmas story. Yet his task was an important component of God's incredible plan. As we read the story of the birth of Jesus, we find that Joseph was just, righteous, merciful, protective, and courageous. But most of all—he was obedient. When the angel told him to take Mary as his wife, he obeyed (Matthew 1:24). And when the angel told him to flee to Egypt with Mary and Jesus, he did (2:13–14).

Just as Mary was carefully chosen to bear the Son of God, Joseph was deliberately chosen to provide for his young wife and the Christ-child. And trusting God, Joseph followed through on everything God asked him to do.

What is God asking of you today? Are you willing to com-mit yourself to do whatever He wants you to do?

We can learn much about obedience from Joseph, the for-gotten man of Christmas. —CINDY KASPER

The Facts of Life

After this his wife Elizabeth became pregnant and for five months remained in seclusion. "The LORD has done this for me," she said. "In these days he has shown his favor and taken away my disgrace among the people."

In the sixth month, God sent the angel Gabriel to Nazareth, a town in Galilee, to a virgin pledged to be married to a man named Joseph, a descendant of David. The virgin's name was Mary. The angel went to her and said, "Greetings, you who are highly favored! The Lord is with you."

Mary was greatly troubled at his words and wondered what kind of greeting this might be. But the angel said to her, "Do not be afraid, Mary, you have found favor with God. You will be with child and give birth to a son, and you are to give him the name Jesus. He will be great and will be called the Son of the Most High. The LORD God will give him the throne of his father David, and he will reign over the house of Jacob forever; his kingdom will never end." . . .

"I am the LORD's servant," Mary answered. "May it be to me as you have said." Then the angel left her. —LUKE 1:24–33, 38

*I*t seems that most of our struggles revolve around wanting something we don't have or having something we don't want. Our deepest longings and our greatest challenges are deeply rooted in trying to see the hand of God in these two facts of life. This is where Luke's account of the birth of Jesus begins.

The aging Elizabeth longed for a baby. For the young and engaged Mary, however, pregnancy should have been a disgrace. But when both learned they would have a child, they accepted the news with faith in the God whose timing is perfect and for whom nothing is impossible (Luke 1:24–25, 37–38).

As we read the Christmas story, we may be struck by the real-life context of the people whose names have become so familiar. Even while Zechariah and Elizabeth suffered their culture's stigma of childlessness, they were described as "upright in the sight of God, observing all the LORD's commandments and regulations blamelessly" (v. 6). And the angel told Mary she had found favor with God (v. 30).

Their example shows us the value of a trusting heart that accepts the mysterious ways of God and the presence of His mighty hand, no matter how perplexing our circumstances may be.   —DAVID MCCASLAND

The Blessing Tree

And Mary said:
"My soul glorifies the LORD
    and my spirit rejoices in God my Savior,
for he has been mindful
    of the humble state of his servant.
From now on all generations will call me blessed,
    for the Mighty One has done great things for me—
        holy is his name.
His mercy extends to those who fear him,
    from generation to generation.
He has performed mighty deeds with his arm;
    he has scattered those who are proud in their inmost
        thoughts.
He has brought down rulers from their thrones
    but has lifted up the humble.
He has filled the hungry with good things
    but has sent the rich away empty.
He has helped his servant Israel,
    remembering to be merciful
to Abraham and his descendants forever,
    even as he said to our fathers."

—LUKE 1:46–55

read about a young couple whose business had failed, and they had little money to spend at Christmas. They were going to have to move out of their house after the new year. But they didn't want their holiday season to be spoiled because of it. So they decided to throw a party. When the guests arrived, they saw a cedar tree decorated with one string of lights and small rolled-up pieces of paper tied to the limbs with ribbon.

"Welcome to our 'blessing tree'!" they said, beaming. "In spite of hard times, God has blessed us in so many ways that we decided to dedicate our tree to Him. Each piece of paper describes a blessing He has given us this year."

This couple has faced more trials since then, but they have chosen to stay focused on the LORD. They often remark that the Christmas with the "blessing tree" was one of their most beautiful, because they could testify as Mary did: "My spirit rejoices in God my Savior . . . for the Mighty One has done great things for me" (Luke 1:47–49).

Whatever your difficulties, they needn't spoil Christmas, for nothing can spoil Christ! Stay focused on Jesus and seek ways to share His blessings with others—perhaps through your own "blessing tree."　　　　　　　　　　—JOANIE YODER

Door of Humility

Your attitude should be the same as that of Christ Jesus:
Who, being in very nature God,
did not consider equality with God something to
be grasped,
but made himself nothing,
taking the very nature of a servant,
being made in human likeness.
And being found in appearance as a man,
he humbled himself
and became obedient to death—
even death on a cross!
Therefore God exalted him to the highest place
and gave him the name that is above every name,
that at the name of Jesus every knee should bow,
in heaven and on earth and under the earth,
and every tongue confess that Jesus Christ is LORD,
to the glory of God the Father.

—PHILIPPIANS 2:5–11

Over the centuries, the entrance to Bethlehem's Church of the Nativity has twice been made smaller. The purpose in the last case was to keep marauders from entering the basilica on horseback. It's now referred to as the "Door of Humility," because visitors must bend down to enter.

As we age, bending our knees becomes more and more difficult and painful. In the physical realm, some people courageously undergo knee replacement surgery. To avoid years of increasingly painful joint damage, they endure several weeks of agony.

Like physical knees, spiritual knees can grow stiff over time. Years of stubborn pride and selfishness make us inflexible, and it becomes increasingly difficult and painful for us to humble ourselves. Seduced by false feelings of importance when others submit to us, we never learn that true importance comes from submitting ourselves to God and to others (Ephesians 5:21; 1 Peter 5:5).

As we celebrate Jesus' birth, it's good to remember the Door of Humility, for it reminds us that we all need new knees—knees that will bend. Humbly is the only way to enter the presence of God.

What better way to honor the One who bent so low to be with us.   —JULIE ACKERMAN LINK

A Real Christmas

Now there was a man in Jerusalem called Simeon, who was righteous and devout. He was waiting for the consolation of Israel, and the Holy Spirit was upon him. It had been revealed to him by the Holy Spirit that he would not die before he had seen the LORD's Christ. Moved by the Spirit, he went into the temple courts. When the parents brought in the child Jesus to do for him what the custom of the Law required, Simeon took him in his arms and praised God, saying:

> *"Sovereign LORD, as you have promised,*
> *you now dismiss your servant in peace.*
> *For my eyes have seen your salvation,*
> *which you have prepared in the sight of all people,*
> *a light for revelation to the Gentiles*
> *and for glory to your people Israel."*

The child's father and mother marveled at what was said about him. Then Simeon blessed them and said to Mary, his mother: "This child is destined to cause the falling and rising of many in Israel, and to be a sign that will be spoken against, so that the thoughts of many hearts will be revealed. And a sword will pierce your own soul too." —LUKE 2:25–35

A quotation in our church's Advent devotional guide caused me to rethink my approach to Christmas:

"Let us at all costs avoid the temptation to make our Christmas worship a withdrawal from the stress and sorrow of life into a realm of unreal beauty. It was into the real world that Christ came, into the city where there was no room for Him, and into a country where Herod, the murderer of innocents, was king.

"He comes to us, not to shield us from the harshness of the world but to give us the courage and strength to bear it; not to snatch us away by some miracle from the conflict of life, but to give us peace—His peace—in our hearts, by which we may be calmly steadfast while the conflict rages, and be able to bring to the torn world the healing that is peace."

When Mary and Joseph presented the infant Jesus to the LORD, Simeon said to them: "This child is destined to cause the falling and rising of many in Israel, and to be a sign that will be spoken against, so that the thoughts of many hearts will be revealed. And a sword will pierce your own soul too" (Luke 2:34–35).

Christmas is not a retreat from reality but an advance into it alongside the Prince of Peace.　　　—DAVID McCASLAND

Pondering the Birth of Christ

When the angels had left them and gone into heaven, the shepherds said to one another, "Let's go to Bethlehem and see this thing that has happened, which the LORD has told us about."

So they hurried off and found Mary and Joseph, and the baby, who was lying in the manger. When they had seen him, they spread the word concerning what had been told them about this child, and all who heard it were amazed at what the shepherds said to them. But Mary treasured up all these things and pondered them in her heart. The shepherds returned, glorifying and praising God for all the things they had heard and seen, which were just as they had been told. —LUKE 2:15–20

*M*any wonder at the things which occurred in Bethlehem centuries ago, but few take the time to really ponder their deeper meaning.

Let us take time today to look at a few interesting facts pertaining to the Savior, and, like Mary, also contemplate their blessed significance. To begin with, Andrew Murray, viewing Luke 2 in the light of Colossians 1, gives us this startling comment on which we may meditate: "Jesus was born twice! His coming to Bethlehem was a birth into a life of weakness. Later, however, as 'the first-born from the dead' (Colossians 1:18), He arose from the grave in the power and glory of Heaven and ascended to the Throne."

Note also the following facts: The shepherds were willing to leave their sheep because they were more interested in viewing "the Lamb of God, who takes away the sin of the world" (John 1:29). The wisemen, having worshiped the young child Jesus, "returned to their country by another route" (Matthew 2:12). So too, after bowing before Christ as Savior and LORD, we can no longer walk the broad avenues we once trod but must go "another way" to journey home. Giving the LORD our consecrated devotion and gifts—as did the Magi—we ought then to take Him into the arms of our faith, loving Him like the ancient Simeon, and speaking of Him to others as did the prophetess Anna.

With Mary we should prayerfully ponder these and the many other blessed truths surrounding Christ's birth, and then adore God for "so great salvation"!   —HENRY BOSCH

One Hundred Percent Right

We did not follow cleverly invented stories when we told you about the power and coming of our LORD Jesus Christ, but we were eyewitnesses of his majesty. For he received honor and glory from God the Father when the voice came to him from the Majestic Glory, saying, "This is my Son, whom I love; with him I am well pleased." We ourselves heard this voice that came from heaven when we were with him on the sacred mountain.

And we have the word of the prophets made more certain, and you will do well to pay attention to it, as to a light shining in a dark place, until the day dawns and the morning star rises in your hearts. Above all, you must understand that no prophecy of Scripture came about by the prophet's own interpretation. For prophecy never had its origin in the will of man, but men spoke from God as they were carried along by the Holy Spirit.

—2 PETER 1:16–21

It's amazing what can be done with statistics. By a clever arrangement of facts, framed in a shrewdly worded context, it is possible to make even a poor situation sound good. For example, a weatherman once boasted, "I'm 90 percent right—10 percent of the time!" By contrast, however, the Bible's predictions are 100 percent right.

The LORD Jesus was born in the city of Bethlehem (Micah 5:2); of a virgin (Isaiah 7:14); at the time specified by Daniel (Daniel 9:25). Infants in Bethlehem were massacred as foretold by Jeremiah (Jeremiah 31:15); Jesus went down into Egypt and returned as prophesied by Hosea (Hosea 11:1). Isaiah foretold His ministry in Galilee (Isaiah 9:1, 2); Zechariah predicted His triumphal entry into Jerusalem riding upon a colt (Zechariah 9:9), His betrayal for thirty pieces of silver (11:12); and the return of this money for the purchase of a potter's field (11:13). David lived one thousand years before the birth of Christ and had never seen a Roman crucifixion; yet in Psalm 22, he penned under divine inspiration a graphic portrayal of the death Jesus suffered. Isaiah 53 also gives us a detailed picture of our LORD's rejection, maltreatment, death, and burial. These few prophecies (and there are many more) should impress the worst of skeptics with the reliability of the Bible.

Since these predictions have all been fulfilled to the smallest detail, let us also accept with confidence that which the Bible says about the future. Remember, we have a sure word of prophecy which is 100 percent right—all of the time!

—RICHARD DE HAAN

The Christ Has Come!

And there were shepherds living out in the fields nearby, keeping watch over their flocks at night. An angel of the LORD appeared to them, and the glory of the LORD shone around them, and they were terrified. But the angel said to them, "Do not be afraid. I bring you good news of great joy that will be for all the people. Today in the town of David a Savior has been born to you; he is Christ the LORD. This will be a sign to you: You will find a baby wrapped in cloths and lying in a manger."

Suddenly a great company of the heavenly host appeared with the angel, praising God and saying,

"Glory to God in the highest,
and on earth peace to men on whom his favor rests."

—LUKE 2:8–14

*T*he birth of the LORD Jesus Christ was right on schedule as far as God's calendar was concerned. The Bible tells us in Galatians 4:4 that "when the time had fully come, God sent his Son, born of a woman." From man's viewpoint, however, the Savior's appearance seemed long overdue. Talmage expresses it this way: "How painfully and wearily one thousand years of the world's existence rolled along and no Christ. Two thousand years and no Christ. Three thousand years and no Christ. Four thousand years and no Christ. 'Give us a Christ,' had cried the Assyrian and Persian and Chaldean and Egyptian civilizations, but the lips of the earth and the lips of the sky made no answer. However, the slow century and the slow year and the slow month and the slow hour at last arrived. The world had enjoyed concerts in the morning and vespers in the evening, but now it was to have a concert at midnight. The window shutters of night were thrown open. Some of the best singers stood there, and pulling back the drapery of cloud, they chanted a peace anthem until all the echoes from hill and valley applauded and encored the 'Hallelujah Chorus.' "

Today with them we would join our happy voices in grateful retrospect as we raise the glad carol, "O little town of Bethlehem, how still we see thee lie! Above thy deep and dreamless sleep the silent stars go by. Yet in thy dark streets shineth the everlasting Light; the hopes and fears of all the years are met in thee tonight." Yes, thank God, the Christ has come!

—RICHARD DE HAAN

Christmas Is for Everyone!

There was also a prophetess, Anna, the daughter of Phanuel, of the tribe of Asher. She was very old; she had lived with her husband seven years after her marriage, and then was a widow until she was eighty-four. She never left the temple but worshiped night and day, fasting and praying. Coming up to them at that very moment, she gave thanks to God and spoke about the child to all who were looking forward to the redemption of Jerusalem.

—LUKE 2:36–38

*T*he tragic commercialization of Christmas has caused some adults to become so overwhelmed with activity that they feel it is a time of happiness only for children. While this may be true in the secular sense, it does not apply to the real meaning of the season. The birth of Jesus should fill the hearts of everyone with joy; for the aged and the young, the wealthy and the poor, the strong and the weak all need the salvation He came to provide.

One of those most thrilled by the promised Messiah's arrival was an aged widow. She had lost her husband and the physical bloom of youth; yet she kept on believing, continued to worship, and never ceased to pray. Entering the temple one day, she saw the Baby Jesus in the arms of Simeon. She instantly knew that He was the Christ and immediately gave fervent thanks to God.

Certainly the coming of Jesus Christ into the world is good news for children. It tells them that God has provided for their redemption from sin, and promises them that the LORD will be with them throughout their lives and forever. But it is also a wonderful event for adults. It assures them that they need not fear death, because our Savior came, paid the price for sin, and destroyed the power of the grave. The young should therefore take their eyes off the tinsel and toys of Christmas to praise God for the gift of His Son, and the aged should likewise give "thanks . . . unto the LORD." Let us all become less occupied with the gifts, the activities, and the expenses of the Christmas season, and pause to reflect upon the One who came to save us.

—HERB VANDER LUGT

It's a Fact

In the beginning was the Word, and the Word was with God, and the Word was God. He was with God in the beginning.

Through him all things were made; without him nothing was made that has been made. In him was life, and that life was the light of men. The light shines in the darkness, but the darkness has not understood it . . .

He was in the world, and though the world was made through him, the world did not recognize him. He came to that which was his own, but his own did not receive him. Yet to all who received him, to those who believed in his name, he gave the right to become children of God—children born not of natural descent, nor of human decision or a husband's will, but born of God.

The Word became flesh and made his dwelling among us. We have seen his glory, the glory of the One and Only, who came from the Father, full of grace and truth. —JOHN 1:1–5, 10–14

I can well remember my reaction as a child when I heard for the first time that December 25 might not be the actual day of our Savior's birth. The thought came to me, how can we really celebrate His birthday if we don't know exactly when He was born? As time went on, I came to realize that it's not the date but the fact of His incarnation that counts. And no one who is willing to read the Scriptures with an open mind can escape the deeper meaning that "the Word became flesh, and made his dwelling among us" (John 1:14). What's important is that the Savior really did come into this world as a man. It makes no difference whether it was December 25, January 6, April 20, or November 20.

Look again at the record. The account of Jesus' birth includes details that any informed individual would recognize as reliable. The swaddling clothes, the inn, the shepherds' visit all support the conclusion that the Son of God did indeed enter this space-time world. There is no question about it. He did come. He did live a perfect life. He did die a sacrificial death. He did rise from the dead! These things are undeniable, and any open-minded person will acknowledge them as true. Remember, the exact date when our LORD was born is really quite incidental, but the fact that Jesus came to dwell on this planet means everything.

How fitting, then, that we pause at this season of the year to praise God for the gift of His love. Along with believers around the world, let us be thankful that Christ has come. That is a fact!

—RICHARD DE HAAN

Light Overcoming Darkness

Herod called the Magi secretly and found out from them the exact time the star had appeared. He sent them to Bethlehem and said, "Go and make a careful search for the child. As soon as you find him, report to me, so that I too may go and worship him."

After they had heard the king, they went on their way, and the star they had seen in the east went ahead of them until it stopped over the place where the child was. When they saw the star, they were overjoyed. On coming to the house, they saw the child with his mother Mary, and they bowed down and worshiped him . . . And having been warned in a dream not to go back to Herod, they returned to their country by another route.

When they had gone, an angel of the LORD appeared to Joseph in a dream. "Get up," he said, "take the child and his mother and escape to Egypt. Stay there until I tell you, for Herod is going to search for the child to kill him." So he got up, took the child and his mother during the night and left for Egypt, where he stayed until the death of Herod.

—MATTHEW 2:7–15

When Herod realized that he had been outwitted by the Magi, he was furious, and he gave orders to kill all the boys in Bethlehem and its vicinity who were two years old and under, in accordance with the time he had learned from the Magi.

When Herod ordered the massacre in Bethlehem it must have seemed to the sorrowing parents that evil was stronger than the power of God. The Gentile world had become increasingly immoral, and the Hebrew religion had deteriorated into empty legalism. Herod ruthlessly killed anyone who stood in his way, including his wife Mariamme and at least three of his sons. Jewish writers have referred to this period as the midnight hour of their history.

The forces of darkness did not win out, however, for God intervened and protected the Savior by instructing Joseph and Mary to take Him into Egypt. And even though Jesus was later misunderstood and hated, He completely fulfilled God's holy law for us. By dying on a cross to pay the price for human sin and then rising victoriously, He broke the power of death and made eternal salvation available to all who believe.

Once again the horizon is heavy with the ominous clouds of false religions, gross immorality, and widespread despair. But we who are trusting Him can be filled with hope, for the Christmas story reminds us that God will surely prevail! Even as Christ's birth illumined the dark sky of the Greco-Roman world with a new dawn, so His glorious return to this earth will bring about the final triumph of light over darkness. —HERB VANDER LUGT

The Servant of Servants

If you have any encouragement from being united with Christ, if any comfort from his love, if any fellowship with the Spirit, if any tenderness and compassion, then make my joy complete by being like-minded, having the same love, being one in spirit and purpose. Do nothing out of selfish ambition or vain conceit, but in humility consider others better than yourselves. Each of you should look not only to your own interests, but also to the interests of others.

Your attitude should be the same as that of Christ Jesus.

—PHILIPPIANS 2:1–5

Today's Scripture indicates that our attitude toward others should be shaped by the infinite sacrifice we see in the incarnation. When our LORD set aside heaven's glory, He became the Servant of servants. If our celebration of the birth of Mary's firstborn Son does not soften and sensitize our feelings toward one another, we may be using the occasion of Christmas as an excuse for a selfish kind of giving and receiving.

As we review what the Son of God gave up when He came to this earth, we should remember this: one who suffers little does not groan in the presence of one who suffers much. For instance, would it be appropriate to complain bitterly about chapped hands while visiting a leprosarium where people have knobby stubs at the end of their arms? What kind of man would whine about sore feet to a person who had no feet at all? Or what sensitive citizen would cry about having to pay taxes while standing at the graveside of one who had given his life for his country?

In an infinitely greater way we should think seriously about the birth of Christ, for it represents the beginning of an ultimate sacrifice that makes all our petty inconveniences fade into insignificance. The eternal God humbled Himself and became a man who lived and died for us. What right have we, then, to complain when He commands us to serve one another? This lesson may be difficult to accept but it's at the very heart of the incarnation. To commemorate Christ's birth properly, we must become a servant of the Servant of servants! —MART DE HAAN

Bethlehem's Innkeeper

In those days Caesar Augustus issued a decree that a census should be taken of the entire Roman world. (This was the first census that took place while Quirinius was governor of Syria.) And everyone went to his own town to register.

So Joseph also went up from the town of Nazareth in Galilee to Judea, to Bethlehem the town of David, because he belonged to the house and line of David. He went there to register with Mary, who was pledged to be married to him and was expecting a child. While they were there, the time came for the baby to be born, and she gave birth to her firstborn, a son. She wrapped him in cloths and placed him in a manger, because there was no room for them in the inn. —LUKE 2:1–7 *f* the innkeeper of Bethlehem had known that Mary was to give birth to the Messiah that night, do you suppose he would have done more to provide for her? No doubt he would have moved out of his own quarters and allowed her to occupy his room rather than a stable. If he had, what a blessing he would have received! Not only would he have known the joy of having given his all to the Savior, but I believe he would have been invited to share in the intimate fellowship of those who were privileged to behold the newborn King.

Thomas Lambie and several others once visited the Palestinian fields where the shepherds tended their flocks long ago. As they walked along, they sang, "Joy to the world! The LORD is come! Let earth receive her King; let every heart prepare Him room." Dr. Lambie commented later that these words reminded him of missionaries in India who were friends of a government official. Whenever the viceroy came to their town on business, they would vacate their home, leaving it completely to him. His first act after moving in was to ask the missionaries to return as his guests. By giving their best to this leader, they were able to enjoy his company and hospitality.

You and I are in a similar position. We have the privilege of making room in our hearts for the King of kings. We must hold back nothing, giving full control of our lives to Christ. When we do, He graciously bids us come and abide with Him, not for a brief visit but to enjoy His presence for time and eternity. Do you have room for Jesus?　　—PAUL VAN GORDER

That Beautiful Name

This is how the birth of Jesus Christ came about: His mother Mary was pledged to be married to Joseph, but before they came together, she was found to be with child through the Holy Spirit. Because Joseph her husband was a righteous man and did not want to expose her to public disgrace, he had in mind to divorce her quietly.

But after he had considered this, an angel of the LORD appeared to him in a dream and said, "Joseph son of David, do not be afraid to take Mary home as your wife, because what is conceived in her is from the Holy Spirit. She will give birth to a son, and you are to give him the name Jesus, because he will save his people from their sins."

All this took place to fulfill what the LORD had said through the prophet: "The virgin will be with child and will give birth to a son, and they will call him Immanuel"—which means, "God with us."

When Joseph woke up, he did what the angel of the LORD had commanded him and took Mary home as his wife. But he had no union with her until she gave birth to a son. And he gave him the name Jesus.   —MATTHEW 1:18–25

When people say that someone's name is beautiful, they are usually referring to its sound. Parents today seldom choose a name for their children because of its meaning. They pick one that reminds them of a friend or a relative, or they select it because it has a combination of syllables that is pleasing to the ears.

To say that the name Jesus is beautiful is not to speak merely of phonetics. True, the word does have a gracious quality all its own, and even when I hear it spoken in other languages, it has a lovely sound. But its real beauty lies in its deep meaning. In today's Scripture we read that an angel of the LORD appeared to Joseph in a dream and told him Mary's child should be called "Jesus," for He would save His people from their sins. That's why the mention of His name brings to my mind a picture of His entire life—His humble birth, His sinless character, His profound teachings, His atoning death, His bodily resurrection, His glorious ascension, His place at God's right hand, and His second coming. You see, these wonderful truths are all part of His redeeming work for sinners, and they are compressed into that wonderful word "Jesus."

Many names bring pleasant associations to mind, but only one sets my heart aglow. It fills me with gratitude, joy, and hope because of who it represents and what He has done for me. What emotions well up within you when you hear the word "Jesus"? Do you know the joy and peace experienced by all who have called on that beautiful name?   —HERB VANDER LUGT

Sonlight

Through him all things were made; without him nothing was made that has been made. In him was life, and that life was the light of men. The light shines in the darkness, but the darkness has not understood it.

There came a man who was sent from God; his name was John. He came as a witness to testify concerning that light, so that through him all men might believe. He himself was not the light; he came only as a witness to the light. The true light that gives light to every man was coming into the world . . .

The Word became flesh and made his dwelling among us. We have seen his glory, the glory of the One and Only, who came from the Father, full of grace and truth. —JOHN 1:3–9, 14

This day has long been celebrated for its relationship to light. Back in AD 274 an emperor of the old Roman world chose December 25 as "the birthday of the unconquered sun." He recognized that at this midwinter date it reaches its lowest point in the southern sky and begins its gradual movement northward again. The annual rebirth of nature was closely linked to the Roman new year and planting season. Houses were decorated with greenery and candles, and presents were given to children and the poor. In time, Christians made this a holy day of their own. By AD 336, the church had decided that all believers should celebrate the birthday of the LORD Jesus, the Son of righteousness, on December 25.

Although we cannot be certain of the exact date the Savior was born, there is little doubt that most of us, like the Romans, look forward to longer days and warmer weather. But can we say that we are as happy about the coming of the Light into the world? This is a serious and difficult question. The Light from God not only brings the warmth of His love, but also burns. He exposes our pride, our greed, and our lack of self-control. Even though we're His children, it's easier to hide from this brightness than to admit our continual need of His mercy and His strength.

But that is what Christmas is all about. A new day has come! God's Light has been born into the world, and is still shining over us. Today, let's celebrate humbly and gratefully in the light of His Son.　　　　　　　　　　　　—MART DE HAAN

The Miraculous in Christmas

In the sixth month, God sent the angel Gabriel to Nazareth, a town in Galilee, to a virgin pledged to be married to a man named Joseph, a descendant of David. The virgin's name was Mary. The angel went to her and said, "Greetings, you who are highly favored! The LORD is with you."

Mary was greatly troubled at his words and wondered what kind of greeting this might be. But the angel said to her, "Do not be afraid, Mary, you have found favor with God. You will be with child and give birth to a son, and you are to give him the name Jesus. He will be great and will be called the Son of the Most High. The LORD God will give him the throne of his father David, and he will reign over the house of Jacob forever; his kingdom will never end."

—LUKE 1:26–33

I know a minister who talks about God revealed in Christ and uses the traditional Christmas music in his church. But he told me he isn't sure Mary was a virgin when she became the mother of Jesus, and he insists that it's wrong to be dogmatic about His deity. He refers to the "Christmas event," but he's stripped away all its miraculous elements.

I have no problem accepting the supernatural in the story of Jesus' coming into the world. But I do have a question about this man's theology. I don't know why he even celebrates this blessed holiday. If the Savior's birth was not a miracle by which God took upon Himself our humanity to redeem us, then the "Christmas event" is a farce. One must make a choice—either believe everything the New Testament claims about the LORD or admit that we have no gospel to preach. If Jesus were a mere man who died on a cross after a brief three-year ministry, He would not have gained worldwide fame.

A skeptic once taunted, "If I claimed to be God as Jesus did, I could go down in history as a messiah too." A Christian replied, "Yes, if your mother testifies that you were born without a human father, if you live a sinless life, if you let yourself be crucified, and if you rise again the third day and show yourself to a large number of people—then you too could go down in history as a messiah."

Without question, Jesus' incarnation was the greatest miracle the world has ever seen—God in the person of Christ becoming a man to bring us salvation. —HERB VANDER LUGT

A Genuine Gift

This is how the birth of Jesus Christ came about: His mother Mary was pledged to be married to Joseph, but before they came together, she was found to be with child through the Holy Spirit. Because Joseph her husband was a righteous man and did not want to expose her to public disgrace, he had in mind to divorce her quietly.

But after he had considered this, an angel of the LORD appeared to him in a dream and said, "Joseph son of David, do not be afraid to take Mary home as your wife, because what is conceived in her is from the Holy Spirit. She will give birth to a son, and you are to give him the name Jesus, because he will save his people from their sins."

All this took place to fulfill what the LORD had said through the prophet: "The virgin will be with child and will give birth to a son, and they will call him Immanuel"—which means, "God with us."

When Joseph woke up, he did what the angel of the LORD had commanded him and took Mary home as his wife. But he had no union with her until she gave birth to a son. And he gave him the name Jesus. —MATTHEW 1:18–25

A young man who was engaged to marry a lovely girl bought her a diamond ring and placed it on her finger. It was not a very large stone, but it had a brilliant sparkle. One day a jealous, cynical friend looked at it and said, "That's not a genuine diamond—it's merely an imitation." At first the young woman was very distressed. Had her fiancé given her a cheap ring? So she asked her father to take it to a jeweler to ascertain its quality. After careful examination the expert said it was a "pure white diamond of the first water." The woman's confidence in her lover was restored. He would never give her anything that was not genuine.

In the same way, God sent His only begotten Son into the world, and He is called in the Scriptures an "unspeakable gift." He is a priceless treasure. Matthew 1:18–25 records some tremendous statements that present Him as being truly the Son of God. There is nothing phony about Him! He is the Word made flesh. He is the Son of the Eternal One. Verses 18 and 20 state that Mary's child was conceived not by a human father but by the Holy Spirit. Verse 21 shows that the babe was divinely named "Jesus" because He would save His people from their sins. Verses 22 and 23 declare that His birth was the fulfillment of prophecy, and that He came from Heaven to dwell among men.

Take a long look at Jesus, my friend. Behold Him! He is genuine. The sparkle of deity emanates from His person. He was Mary's child, but He is God's Son.

Come, let us adore Him, Christ, the LORD.

—PAUL VAN GORDER

105

Light in Your Darkness

Now there was a man in Jerusalem called Simeon, who was righteous and devout. He was waiting for the consolation of Israel, and the Holy Spirit was upon him. It had been revealed to him by the Holy Spirit that he would not die before he had seen the LORD's Christ. Moved by the Spirit, he went into the temple courts. When the parents brought in the child Jesus to do for him what the custom of the Law required, Simeon took him in his arms and praised God, saying:

> "Sovereign LORD, as you have promised,
>   you now dismiss your servant in peace.
> For my eyes have seen your salvation,
>   which you have prepared in the sight of all people,
> a light for revelation to the Gentiles
>   and for glory to your people Israel."

The child's father and mother marveled at what was said about him. —LUKE 2:25–33

For more than four hundred years no new revelation had come from heaven to brighten the landscape of man's sinful night. Then suddenly darkness gave way to light. Jesus the promised Messiah left the ivory palaces of glory and visited this sin-cursed earth. In His self-sacrificing love He brought grace, mercy, and forgiveness to a lost and dying race.

An artist once made a sketch of a wintry twilight. The trees were laden with snow; and a dreary-looking house, lonely and desolate, stood in the midst of the drifted field. It was a bleak and depressing picture. Then the artist took some yellow chalk and with a few quick strokes put a light in one window of that home. The effect was almost magical. The entire scene was transformed into a vision of comfort and cheer.

Likewise, the birth of Christ brought the luster of hope to this dark world. You'd think people would have rejoiced and eagerly received the Savior. Instead, they lived on in their own dismal depravity, and with wicked hands they crucified the Prince of Life. The second person of the Trinity had come to illuminate them spiritually, but they "loved darkness instead of light, because their deeds were evil" (John 3:19).

On this Christmas Day let us rejoice that Jesus the true Light visited this sin-smitten planet two thousand years ago to cast the joyous rays of His salvation upon our pathway. Now all who bow before Him in repentance and humble adoration—acknowledging Him as Savior and LORD—enjoy the "light of life" that ends earth's darkness forever. —HENRY BOSCH

A Promised Gift

For to us a child is born,
to us a son is given,
and the government will be on his shoulders.
And he will be called
Wonderful Counselor, Mighty God,
Everlasting Father, Prince of Peace.
Of the increase of his government and peace
there will be no end.
He will reign on David's throne
and over his kingdom,
establishing and upholding it
with justice and righteousness
from that time on and forever.
The zeal of the LORD *Almighty*
will accomplish this.

—ISAIAH 9:6–7

*I*n the *Wolf Magazine of Letters,* we read about a woman who in the Christmas rush purchased fifty greeting cards without looking at the message inside. She signed and addressed all but one, and then dropped them in a mailbox, still not taking time to see what they said. The verse on the inside was completely overlooked. Just imagine her dismay when a few days later she glanced at the one unmailed card and read these words:

> This card is just to say
> A little gift is on the way.

Needless to say, that gift was never received by anyone. There were forty-nine disappointed families wondering what had happened to their presents.

How different was God's promise to us! He did send a gift in the person of His Son, the Babe of Bethlehem's manger. You see, many years before the Savior was born, the LORD spoke through the prophet Isaiah, saying, "The virgin will be with child and will give birth to a son, and will call him Immanuel" (Isaiah 7:14). And again in verse 6 of chapter 9 we read, "For to us a child is born, to us a son is given." Did God keep His word? Indeed He did! Galatians 4:4, 5 tells us, "But when the time had fully come, God sent his Son, born of a woman, born under law, to redeem those under law, that we might receive the full rights of sons."

On this special day, as we commemorate the birth of Christ, let's thank God that He meant what He said. He not only promised; He also gave. "Thanks be to God for his indescribable gift" (2 Corinthians 9:15). —RICHARD DE HAAN

Happy Christmas!

"No one has ever gone into heaven except the one who came from heaven—the Son of Man. Just as Moses lifted up the snake in the desert, so the Son of Man must be lifted up, that everyone who believes in him may have eternal life.

"For God so loved the world that he gave his one and only Son, that whoever believes in him shall not perish but have eternal life. For God did not send his Son into the world to condemn the world, but to save the world through him. Whoever believes in him is not condemned, but whoever does not believe stands condemned already because he has not believed in the name of God's one and only Son."   —JOHN 3:13–18

*L*ast Easter morning when I walked into church I saw my friend and greeted her, "Happy Christmas!" I quickly corrected myself. "I mean, Happy Easter!"

"Can't have one without the other," she smiled.

How true! Without Christmas, there wouldn't be an Easter. And without the resurrection, this day would be just another day. In fact, we wouldn't even be in church.

Christmas and Easter are the most joyful celebrations of the year for the Christian. In the first, we celebrate the incarnation (God taking on flesh and coming into the world). "For God so loved the world that he gave his one and only Son . . ." (John 3:16).

In the second, we celebrate Jesus' resurrection. "He is not here; he has risen!" the angel said (Luke 24:6). From the beginning of time, these two days were inextricably linked in the master plan of the Father. Jesus was born to die for our sins and to conquer death so that we could live.

Which is more important? Christmas—the birth of the infant Jesus? Or Easter—the death and resurrection of the man, God's Son? Both are essential—and both are clear evidence of the Father's love for us.

Happy Christmas! And Happy Easter!   —CINDY KASPER

Let Us Adore Him!

And there were shepherds living out in the fields nearby, keeping watch over their flocks at night. An angel of the LORD appeared to them, and the glory of the LORD shone around them, and they were terrified. But the angel said to them, "Do not be afraid. I bring you good news of great joy that will be for all the people. Today in the town of David a Savior has been born to you; he is Christ the LORD. This will be a sign to you: You will find a baby wrapped in cloths and lying in a manger."

Suddenly a great company of the heavenly host appeared with the angel, praising God and saying,

> *"Glory to God in the highest,*
> *and on earth peace to men on whom his favor rests."*

When the angels had left them and gone into heaven, the shepherds said to one another, "Let's go to Bethlehem and see this thing that has happened, which the LORD has told us about."

So they hurried off and found Mary and Joseph, and the baby, who was lying in the manger. When they had seen him, they spread the word concerning what had been told them about this child, and all who heard it were amazed at what the shepherds said to them . . . The shepherds returned, glorifying and praising God for all the things they had heard and seen, which were just as they had been told. —LUKE 2:8–20

In his portrayal of the nativity scene, Rembrandt focuses attention entirely on the Babe in the manger. He does this by depicting a shaft of light that falls exclusively on the Christchild. Though other figures are there, they are shrouded in shadows. Rembrandt knew that to highlight anything else would detract from the wonderful significance of that blessed event.

Luke's gospel gives us a similar picture of Jesus' birth. We are introduced to various people, and the Savior is the focus of their attention. He alone fills their hearts with praise. The virgin Mary magnified the LORD because through the coming of the Messiah His mercy is extended to "those who fear him" (Luke 1:46–50). Zacharias the priest blessed God, declaring, "He has come and has redeemed his people" (Luke 1:68). The shepherds, who were the first to hear the joyful message that the Savior had been born, came and looked upon the baby Jesus, then returned "glorifying and praising God" (Luke 2:20). The devout Simeon, taking the infant into his arms, was zealous in his gratitude and referred to Him as a "light for revelation to the Gentiles and for glory to . . . Israel" (Luke 2:32). And the aged prophetess Anna "spoke of the child to all who were looking forward to the redemption of Jerusalem" (Luke 2:38).

Won't you join in that magnificent chorus of praise which began nearly two thousand years ago on that holy night? Come, let us adore Him, proclaiming joyfully with the angelic host, "Glory to God in the highest, and on earth peace to men on whom his favor rests"! —HENRY BOSCH

Wonder

When the angels had left them and gone into heaven, the shepherds said to one another, "Let's go to Bethlehem and see this thing that has happened, which the LORD has told us about."

So they hurried off and found Mary and Joseph, and the baby, who was lying in the manger. When they had seen him, they spread the word concerning what had been told them about this child, and all who heard it were amazed at what the shepherds said to them. But Mary treasured up all these things and pondered them in her heart. The shepherds returned, glorifying and praising God for all the things they had heard and seen, which were just as they had been told. —LUKE 2:15–20

Elmer Kline, a bakery manager in 1921, was given the job of naming the company's new loaf of bread. As he struggled to come up with something "catchy," he found his answer in an unlikely place. While visiting the grounds of the Indianapolis Motor Speedway, he stopped to watch the International Balloon Festival.

Later he described the sight of the beautiful hot-air balloons launching into the Indiana sky as one of "awe and wonderment." The thought stuck, and he called the new product Wonder Bread. To this day, the packaging for Wonder Bread is brightened by colorful balloons.

Wonder, however, is a word that evokes something more significant than a loaf of bread or hot-air balloons. One dictionary defines wonder as "a cause of astonishment or admiration." It's a word that captures the experience of all the people surrounding the events of the coming of Jesus into the world—the angels, Mary, Joseph, the shepherds, and all the people they told. Luke said they were "amazed" (2:18). For all of them, trying to understand the birth of Christ was an exercise in wonder.

As we celebrate Christmas, may we be filled with wonder at His love and His coming!　　　　　—BILL CROWDER

Two Bethlehems

In the sixth month, God sent the angel Gabriel to Nazareth, a town in Galilee, to a virgin pledged to be married to a man named Joseph, a descendant of David. The virgin's name was Mary. The angel went to her and said, "Greetings, you who are highly favored! The LORD is with you."

Mary was greatly troubled at his words and wondered what kind of greeting this might be. But the angel said to her, "Do not be afraid, Mary, you have found favor with God. You will be with child and give birth to a son, and you are to give him the name Jesus. He will be great and will be called the Son of the Most High. The LORD God will give him the throne of his father David, and he will reign over the house of Jacob forever; his kingdom will never end."

"How will this be," Mary asked the angel, "since I am a virgin?" The angel answered, "The Holy Spirit will come upon you, and the power of the Most High will overshadow you. So the holy one to be born will be called the Son of God.

—LUKE 1:26–35

The birth of Jesus Christ was unlike any other. Mary's was an "other world" conception. The angel told her, "The Holy Spirit will come upon you, and the power of the Most High will overshadow you" (Luke 1:35). The child conceived in her was from outside our world. And it had to be so, because the boy born to Mary was Immanuel, "God with us" (Isaiah 7:14; Matthew 1:23).

The baby born in Bethlehem was of heavenly origin. God had entered the earth in the form and nature of Mary's little son. He came into the world from above, and His incarnation made possible our redemption.

Now think about it. Our own new birth—our regeneration—comes from outside the world. Jesus said that we are born again "of the Spirit" (John 3:3, 7–8). Our salvation is not from an earthly source, but from God Himself through Jesus by means of His Spirit. In a sense, then, our heart becomes a "Bethlehem stable," a place where Jesus comes into the world. We open the door to Him by faith, and He is born in us by the blessed Holy Spirit.

We make Him known to others by His power in us. He affects every aspect of our lives. We are a "Bethlehem," His place of entrance into today's world.   —DAVE EGNER

Touched at Christmas

At that time the disciples came to Jesus and asked, "Who is the greatest in the kingdom of heaven?"

He called a little child and had him stand among them. And he said: "I tell you the truth, unless you change and become like little children, you will never enter the kingdom of heaven. Therefore, whoever humbles himself like this child is the greatest in the kingdom of heaven.

"And whoever welcomes a little child like this in my name welcomes me. But if anyone causes one of these little ones who believe in me to sin, it would be better for him to have a large millstone hung around his neck and to be drowned in the depths of the sea.

"Woe to the world because of the things that cause people to sin! Such things must come, but woe to the man through whom they come! . . ."

Then little children were brought to Jesus for him to place his hands on them and pray for them. But the disciples rebuked those who brought them.

Jesus said, "Let the little children come to me, and do not hinder them, for the kingdom of heaven belongs to such as these." When he had placed his hands on them, he went on from there.

—MATTHEW 18:1–7; 19:13–15

In the past I've been annoyed by crowded church services during the Christmas season. I disliked the jam-packed pews and the hard-to-find parking places. I've even grumbled after being shunted to an overflow room when the sanctuary had filled long before the service began. Why don't these people who come once a year just stay home? I thought.

My attitude seemed to mirror that of the disciples, who scolded those who brought children to Jesus for His blessing (Matthew 19:13). Whatever the reasons, the disciples must have thought they had no right to be there. But Jesus said, "Let the little children come to me, and do not hinder them, the kingdom of heaven belongs to such as these" (v. 14).

I finally came to realize that it's a good thing whenever a person is drawn to a gathering that celebrates Jesus' birth. Whether it's a children's program, a candlelight service, or a concert by the choir, we never know when someone will encounter Christ the LORD. Broadcast journalist Harry Reasoner once said: "So if a Christian is touched only once a year, the touching is still worth it, and maybe on some given Christmas, some quiet morning, the touch will take."

Christmas seems to bring out the child in all of us. And every child is welcomed by Jesus.　　—DAVID McCASLAND

Born to Die

This is how the birth of Jesus Christ came about: His mother Mary was pledged to be married to Joseph, but before they came together, she was found to be with child through the Holy Spirit. Because Joseph her husband was a righteous man and did not want to expose her to public disgrace, he had in mind to divorce her quietly.

But after he had considered this, an angel of the LORD appeared to him in a dream and said, "Joseph son of David, do not be afraid to take Mary home as your wife, because what is conceived in her is from the Holy Spirit. She will give birth to a son, and you are to give him the name Jesus, because he will save his people from their sins."

All this took place to fulfill what the LORD had said through the prophet: "The virgin will be with child and will give birth to a son, and they will call him Immanuel"—which means, "God with us."

When Joseph woke up, he did what the angel of the LORD had commanded him and took Mary home as his wife. But he had no union with her until she gave birth to a son. And he gave him the name Jesus.

—MATTHEW 1:18–25

*A*lthough millions celebrate Jesus' birthday, few seem to be aware of its real significance.

We recognize that His birth was unusual because He was born of a virgin. His life was unique too, for He was the only one who lived without sinning. His death was also unusual. Jesus was not a martyr. He was not the victim of unfortunate circumstances, dying for a worthy cause. Nor did He lay down His life just to set a good example. There's much more to it than that. The LORD Jesus came into this world to be our Savior!

Jesus Himself said that He came "to seek and to save what was lost" (Luke 19:10). Who are the lost? The Bible tells us that "all have sinned" and that "the wages of sin is death" (Romans 3:23; 6:23). In order to save the world, Jesus had to die for it. He came and lived the perfect life and then died the death we should have died. The true meaning of Christmas is that Jesus was born to die. Because He was crucified and then rose from the dead, forgiveness of sin and assurance of heaven is now offered to all who believe (John 1:12).

Have you accepted God's gift of salvation? If not, do so today, and this will be your most meaningful Christmas ever.

—RICHARD DE HAAN

Praiseworthy

Then I saw a Lamb, looking as if it had been slain, standing in the center of the throne, encircled by the four living creatures and the elders . . . And they sang a new song:

> *"You are worthy to take the scroll*
> *   and to open its seals,*
> *because you were slain,*
> *   and with your blood you purchased men for God*
> *   from every tribe and language and people and nation."*
> *   . . .*

Then I looked and heard the voice of many angels, . . . They encircled the throne and the living creatures and the elders. In a loud voice they sang:

> *"Worthy is the Lamb, who was slain,*
> *to receive power and wealth and wisdom and strength*
> *and honor and glory and praise!"*

Then I heard every creature in heaven and on earth and under the earth and on the sea, and all that is in them, singing:

> *"To him who sits on the throne and to the Lamb*
> *be praise and honor and glory and power,*
> *   for ever and ever!"*

—REVELATION 5:6, 9, 11–13

The Grand Rapids Symphony Orchestra and Symphonic Choir were presenting their annual Christmas concert. Near the conclusion, they were joined by the four thousand members of the audience in singing: "Joy to the world, the LORD is come! Let earth receive her King." I got chills when we sang the words, "And heaven and nature sing."

Despite the magnificence of that moment, it was but a faint shadow of the praise that will be raised to the Lamb in heaven. Jesus is worthy of the adoration and praise of all beings: "Worthy is the Lamb, who was slain, to receive power and wealth and wisdom and strength and honor and glory and praise!" (Revelation 5:12).

In Revelation 5, we read John's description of a widening circle of praise to the LORD. It begins with "four living creatures and the twenty-four elders" (v. 8). They are joined by angels numbering "ten thousand times ten thousand" (v. 11).

But that's not all. Every creature in heaven, on earth, and in the sea will one day sing, "To him who sits on the throne and to the Lamb be praise and honor and glory and power, for ever and ever!" (v. 13).

You don't have to wait for that day to sing praise to the Lamb. He is worthy of your praise right now! —DAVE EGNER

Down from His Glory

In the beginning was the Word, and the Word was with God, and the Word was God. He was with God in the beginning.

Through him all things were made; without him nothing was made that has been made. In him was life, and that life was the light of men. The light shines in the darkness, but the darkness has not understood it . . .

He was in the world, and though the world was made through him, the world did not recognize him. He came to that which was his own, but his own did not receive him. Yet to all who received him, to those who believed in his name, he gave the right to become children of God—children born not of natural descent, nor of human decision or a husband's will, but born of God.

The Word became flesh and made his dwelling among us. We have seen his glory, the glory of the One and Only, who came from the Father, full of grace and truth. —JOHN 1:1–5, 10–14

The land of Persia was once ruled by a wise and beloved Shah who cared greatly for his people and desired only what was best for them. One day he disguised himself as a poor man and went to visit the public baths. The water for the baths was heated by a furnace in the cellar, so the Shah made his way to that dark place to sit with the man who tended the fire. The two men shared coarse food, and the Shah befriended the man in his loneliness. Day after day the ruler went to visit the man. The worker became attached to this stranger because he "came where he was" (Luke 10:33). One day the Shah revealed his true identity, and he expected the man to ask him for a gift. Instead, he looked long into his leader's face and with love and wonder in his voice said, "You left your palace and your glory to sit with me in this dark place, to eat my coarse food, and to care about what happens to me. On others you may bestow rich gifts, but to me you have given yourself!"

As we think of what our LORD has done for us, we can echo that fire tender's sentiments. Oh, what a step our LORD took—from heaven to earth, from the worship of angels to the mocking of cruel men, from glory to humiliation! To provide our salvation, Jesus came in human flesh, took upon Himself the form of a servant, and "became obedient to death—even death on a cross" (Philippians 2:8). What a sacrifice—our great Creator became our Savior! Surely He deserves our heartfelt worship and humble adoration. —PAUL VAN GORDER

About the Authors

Henry Bosch served as the first editor of the daily devotional booklet that became *Our Daily Bread* (ODB) and contributed many of the earliest articles. He was also one of the singers on the Radio Bible Class live broadcast.

Dave Branon has done freelance writing for many years and has published more than thirteen books. Dave taught English and coached basketball and baseball at the high school level before coming to RBC Ministries (RBC), where he is now the Managing Editor of *Sports Spectrum* magazine.

Bill Crowder spent over twenty years in pastoral ministry and is now Director of Church Ministries and Director of Publications for RBC Ministries. Bill is the author of *The Spotlight of Faith, The Path of His Passion*, and *Overcoming Life's Challenges*.

Dennis De Haan is a nephew of RBC founder Dr. M. R. De Haan. He pastored two churches in Iowa and Michigan before joining the RBC staff in 1971. He served as the Associate Editor of ODB from 1973 until 1982 and then as Editor until June 1995. Now retired, Dennis continues editing for ODB on a part-time basis.

Mart De Haan is the grandson of RBC founder Dr. M. R. De Haan, and the son of former president, Richard W. De Haan. Mart is the president of RBC Ministries and is heard regularly on the *Discover the Word* radio program and seen on *Day of Discovery* television. Mart is also a contributing writer for ODB, the Discovery Series Bible study booklets, and a monthly column on timely issues called "Been Thinking About."

Richard De Haan was President of RBC Ministries and teacher on RBC programs for twenty years. He was the son of RBC founder, Dr. M. R. De Haan, and wrote a number of full-length books and study booklets for RBC. Often called "the encourager," Richard was committed to faithfulness to God's Word and to integrity as a ministry. Richard went to be with the Lord in 2002.

Dave Egner is now retired from RBC. He was (until June 2002) Managing Editor of *Campus Journal*. He has written Discovery Series study booklets and articles for a variety of publications. Dave taught English and writing for ten years at Grand Rapids Baptist College (now Cornerstone University) before coming to RBC.

Vernon Grounds, Chancellor of Denver Seminary, has had an extensive preaching, teaching, and counseling ministry and was president of Denver Seminary. In addition to writing articles for ODB, he has also written many books and magazine articles.

Cindy Kasper has served at RBC for more than thirty years, most recently as Associate Editor for *Our Journey*. She's an experienced author, having written youth devotional articles for more than a decade.

Julie Ackerman Link is a seasoned writer and editor who has worked on many projects for RBC Ministries and Discovery House Publishers, including the Loving God series. She has been writing for *Our Daily Bread* since December 2000.

David McCasland researches and helps develop biographical documentaries for *Day of Discovery* television, in addition to writing ODB articles. His books include the award-winning biography *Oswald Chambers: Abandoned to God*, a compilation of *The Complete Works of Oswald Chambers*, and *Pure Gold*, a biography of Eric Liddell.

Haddon Robinson is the discussion leader for the RBC Ministries' *Discover the Word* radio program, in addition to writing for *Our Daily Bread*. Dr. Robinson teaches at Gordon-Conwell Theological

Seminary, where he is the Harold J. Ockenga Distinguished Professor of Preaching. He has authored several books, including *Biblical Preaching* and *Biblical Sermons*.

David Roper was a pastor for more than thirty years and now directs Idaho Mountain Ministries, a retreat dedicated to the encouragement of pastoral couples. He is the author of eleven books, including *Psalm 23: The Song of a Passionate Heart*.

Joe Stowell serves as teaching pastor at Harvest Bible Chapel in suburban Chicago. He served for eighteen years as president of Moody Bible Institute, and he now partners with RBC Ministries in radio, writing, and television productions. He has written many books, including *Radical Reliance, Eternity,* and *The Upside of Down*.

Paul Van Gorder began writing regularly for ODB in 1969 and continued until 1992. He also served as associate Bible teacher for the *Day of Discovery* television program and traveled extensively as a speaker for Radio Bible Class. He and his wife now live in retirement in South Carolina.

Herb Vander Lugt remained a vital contributor to *Our Daily Bread* up to the time he went to be with his Lord and Savior on December 2, 2006. He served as Senior Research Editor for RBC Ministries and had been with the ministry since 1966, when he became the third author to contribute to *Our Daily Bread*. In addition to his devotional articles, he wrote numerous Discovery Series booklets and reviewed all study and devotional materials. Herb pastored six churches and held three interim ministerial positions after retiring from the pastorate in 1989.

Joanie Yoder, a favorite among ODB readers, went home to be with her Savior in 2004. She and her husband established a Christian rehabilitation center for drug addicts in England many years ago. Widowed in 1982, she wrote with hope about true dependence on God and his life-changing power.